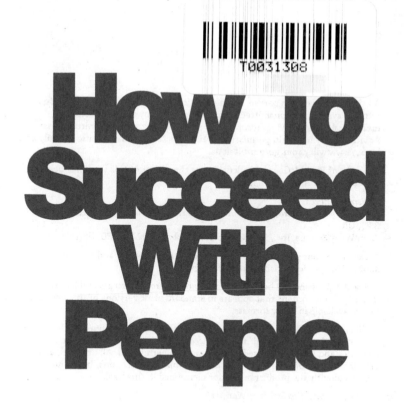

How To Succeed With People

Remarkably Easy Ways to Engage, Influence and Motivate Almost Anyone

Second Edition

Paul McGee

CAPSTONE
A Wiley Brand

This edition first published 2024

Edition History
© 2013 Paul McGee

Registered Offices
John Wiley & Sons Ltd, The Atrium, Southern Gate, Chichester, West Sussex, PO19 8SQ, UK A
John Wiley & Sons, Inc., 111 River Street, Hoboken, NJ 07030, USA

For details of our global editorial offices, customer services, and more information about Wiley products visit us at www.wiley.com.

Wiley also publishes its books in a variety of electronic formats and by print-on-demand. Some content that appears in standard print versions of this book may not be available in other formats.

Library of Congress Cataloging-in-Publication Data is Available:

ISBN 9781394233069 (Paperback)
ISBN 9781394233083 (epdf)
ISBN 9781394233076 (epub)

Cover Design: Wiley
Cover Image: © Fiona Osborne

Set in 11/15pt and Chaparral Pro by Straive, Chennai, India

SKY10070507_032424

"Be curious, not judgmental."

Ted Lasso

Contents

What's the big deal about this people stuff? **vii**

Let's set the scene **1**

SECTION ONE – Stop, Understand **9**

People can't be fixed 11
The mystery of history (part one) 17
The mystery of history (part two) 27
Most people suffer from S.A.D.S. 35
Some people are lightbulbs 41
Why intelligent people do stupid things 47
You get what you tolerate 53
Why change is complicated 61
Humiliation is for amateurs 73
Being nice won't always work 81
It takes two to tango 87
No investment, no return 93

SECTION TWO – Move On **101**

Have realistic expectations 103
Let sleeping dogs lie . . . sometimes 111
Check out your attitude 117

Be willing to be wrong 127
Don't treat people as you want to be treated 135
How to make change a success 141
Four killer questions you have to ask yourself 153
How to make criticism count . . . not crucify 163
Work out why they're whinging 171
How to make people feel S.P.E.C.I.A.L. (part one) 181
How to make people feel S.P.E.C.I.A.L. (part two) 191
How to pick people up when they're feeling down 203
How to talk so people listen 213

The ball's in your court 225

About Paul McGee 235
More Books by Paul McGee 237
Index 239

What's the big deal about this people Stuff?

I wonder if there may be some people you either live or work with who might be secretly or perhaps even publically scoffing at the fact that you're reading this book. Isn't all this stuff better off compartmentalized in the "pink and fluffy" box?

So do they have a point?

Absolutely.

Not.

Let me ask you a few questions.

- Do you know talented people who are currently disengaged and demotivated at work?
- How much does the success of your business depend on the quality of your relationships with customers and clients?
- Are there talented people who've left your organization and the main reason was due to their poor working relationship with their boss?
- Have there been relationships in your personal life that started off well but have now withered and died?
- Does the way you personally handle conflict tend to make things better or worse?
- Are there close family members who no longer speak to each other because of their inability to resolve a conflict?
- Do you know young people who can't wait to leave home because of their relationship with their parents?
- Has your education equipped you with a set of skills necessary to get the best out of yourself and your relationships with others?

Thought-provoking questions eh?

Now let me ask you some more.

So this is all pink and fluffy stuff, right?

It has no real impact on the quality of people's performance at work?

It has no impact on the bottom line?

It has no effect on the quality of your personal relationships?

Yeah right.

If people believe this is just pink and fluffy stuff, what are they?

A comedian?

Deluded?

Scared?

It's time we all got on board the reality train and recognized this:

Bite Size Wisdom

The soft stuff is the serious stuff. It's a big deal

So let's quit playing games that "people are our biggest asset," and then spend hardly any time, energy or resources in equipping them to fulfil their potential. Let's kiss goodbye to tick-box training and sign up to the fact that *we all* need help in knowing how to get the best out of ourselves and others. Especially in these challenging, uncertain and unpredictable times.

Let's ditch this pink and fluffy illusion once and for all, and face facts.

Succeeding with people is a very big deal. And the ability to do so has perhaps never been as important as it is now.

Agree?

What does success mean to you?

Why not press pause for a moment and consider this question:

What does succeeding with people actually mean to you?

Do you hope more people will like you? Listen to you? Buy from you? Agree with you?

Is it a way for you to become more convincing and be more persuasive? Is it about you managing people more effectively or being a better parent? Or is the person you need to get on better with actually yourself?

You see, "success" means different things to different people.

None of us are starting from the same point, or with the same priorities.

So what does it mean for you? How will you know that reading this book has been worthwhile?

What do you want to do more of?

What do you want to do less of?

A lot of people read for pleasure. Fine. But wouldn't it also be worthwhile reading with purpose?

OK, well let's begin by setting the scene, so that you're clear on what you can and cannot expect from reading this book and why I've taken the approach I have in writing it.

Let's Set the Scene

So you've decided to read a book about succeeding with people. Firstly, thanks for choosing this one.

This is actually the second edition, written ten years after the first. It's been fascinating re-reading it and adding to and updating my ideas. And in a world where we're wrestling with the pros and cons of AI (Artificial Intelligence) we still need to develop even more so our PI (People Intelligence).

I genuinely hope you find reading this book to be a valuable investment of your time and helpful on a number of different levels.

To begin with, let me explain why I've written the book and also the reasons I've written it the way I have.

I guess unless you're a recluse or a monk who's taken a vow of silence whilst living in some isolated location, then interacting with people is part of day-to-day life. Despite our rapidly growing relationship with technology, dealing with people in a visible or virtual sense is something few of us can escape.

But here's the deal.

None of us are magically born with a set of skills and insights to deal with the challenges of life and the people we encounter.

Eight billion people currently inhabit this planet, and by 2050 that figure is likely to be around 9 billion. That's a lot of people. Now I know you're not going to meet them all (no matter how big an extrovert you are), but the reality is the number of people you interact with in just a few months of your life is likely to exceed the number your great-grandparents encountered in their entire lifetime.

Throw into the melting pot of those encounters with people economic uncertainty, globalization, information overload, twenty-four/seven living, increased expectations, the rise and role of the internet, the advances of AI, cultural differences and you've got yourself quite a complex concoction.

The bottom line?

Our ancestors never lived in a world even remotely close to the one we're living in now. And whilst there may be an instruction manual for your iPad and your smartphone there isn't one specifically for dealing with people.

Here's the reality.

People are both predictable and unpredictable. Simple and complex. They can be kind. They can be killers. They give. They grab. They're compassionate. They're complacent. They're amazing. They're awful. They love. They hate. They're shaped by their past whilst living in the present.

So I'm not going to give you any bull here. I'm going to tell it as it is.

Faced with such a list of contrasting traits that people possess, the best we can hope for in dealing with them are some really helpful guidelines.

But no guarantees.

Now that's not to say there isn't some good news.

You see, despite the plethora of contradictions that make people who they are, there are some simple ideas, strategies and approaches that will help you build better relationships in both your personal and professional life. There are no magic wands, but they will significantly increase your chances of succeeding with people.

As a professional speaker and coach I've worked in over 40 countries to date, across four continents. And here's one thing I've learnt: Although colour and creed may differ, whether I'm working in America, Africa, Australia, Asia or on my doorstep in Europe, what unites us is greater than what divides us.

In my experience we all have an insatiable drive to improve our lives – sometimes out of necessity, but often driven by our need for security and a sense of purpose.

Most of us want our children to have better lives than our own.

Many of us crave meaning and find it in religion, relationships or belonging to a particular cause or group.

Most of us intuitively know right from wrong.

But there are differences.

Culture, upbringing, age and religion help create those differences and shape our behaviour (I'm particularly fascinated by the way culture influences how we interpret other people's behaviour – for instance, avoiding eye contact in one culture is a sign of respect, but in another it has the opposite effect).

So I want at the outset to acknowledge those differences, and to reassure you I won't be providing a one-size-fits-all approach to dealing with people. However, I do want to raise your awareness and understanding of both yourself and others and provide insights and ideas you can use immediately. Both in and outside of work. Just be aware that you need to tailor them to your own particular situation, culture and current context.

Therefore make sure you use the ideas that are most relevant and realistic for you, recognizing what may work in one situation will fail in another. That's how life and dealing with people is sometimes. So being flexible will be key.

Remember, no matter how good an idea is, it still needs to be used in the right way, in the right context, at the right time. After all . . .

Bite Size Wisdom

A fire extinguisher
could be invaluable.
But it's no use to a
drowning man

Why is the book written the way it is?

There will always be lovers of books. For some people nothing can beat a good novel. But what percentage of the population enjoys wading through a business or self-help book? My guess is it's quite small.

How many people purchase business and self-help books but never finish them?

My guess is quite a lot.

So in an age when we seem cash rich but time poor and where we communicate via blogs and tweets and less through long books I wanted to achieve the best of both worlds.

A book that contains easy bite-size wisdom that won't cause indigestion and can be read in bite-size chunks.

A book that once consumed won't leave you bloated with information but rather energized and inspired with insights and ideas.

Oh, and you'll notice something else.

What you're about to read is both simple and straightforward.

That's deliberate.

My goal is to help you become better at understanding, communicating and connecting with people.

It's not to massage your intellectual ego.

Steve Jobs spent his life trying to make the complex simple. Now I'm no Steve Jobs, but that's what you will find in this book.

Simplicity.

Straightforwardness.

A desire to cut to the chase.

Ideas and insights communicated in a bite-size way.

You will also find honesty. I will share my mistakes and successes, and what I learnt from both.

And you will be challenged. There may be occasions when you're made to feel slightly uncomfortable.

You weren't expecting that, were you?

We like to feel good about ourselves. We like to feel we don't have to do a great deal to achieve success. If you're like me you'd quite like the very act of reading a book to magically transform you.

Beware of that trap. You see, we can delude ourselves into believing that the greater our knowledge the greater our success.

So let me be very straight with you.

I've been on this planet a long time. I've met some very knowledgeable failures. I've met some highly intelligent people who are highly incompetent with people.

Knowledge is a start but it's no guarantee of a successful finish. Neither is having a high IQ.

So along the way expect to be challenged not just to read the book but actually to do something with what you read. However, I promise I'll also include material that will raise the occasional smile. I really do hope you enjoy what you're reading, as well as find yourself being challenged by it at times.

You may also find some chapters more relevant than others. Succeeding with people is a big topic that covers a wide range of issues. Some topics covered are equally important both in and outside of work, but others do have more of a workplace bias.

Hopefully all the content is of interest, but some will be of real importance. So take hold of what is most applicable and perhaps share some of the other ideas with the people around you.

The first section gives you the opportunity to "Stop and Understand" people and to explore what can and can't realistically be achieved in your encounters with others. This includes three brand new chapters, The "mystery of history" parts one and two and a fascinating chapter on change. I think you'll love them and find them incredibly thought provoking in helping you understand yourself and others. The second section helps you to "Move On" by using specific strategies to successfully deal with people in a variety of situations and contexts.

This also includes a new chapter, "How to make change a success." Change is a constant in all our lives and having worked with hundreds of organizations experiencing change, I wanted to give you my take on how to make the process a more positive experience for people, including yourself.

Since this book was first published I've had people from all around the world contact me to share how the ideas you're about to read have helped them. So never underestimate the power and impact of brief and simple ideas to help you on your journey to be successful with people.

But remember this: They're easy to do. They're also easy not to do.

The choice is yours.

Happy reading!

Paul McGee

Section One

Stop, Understand

People can't be fixed

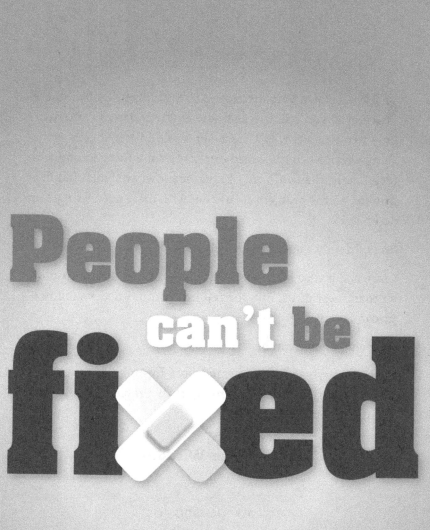

Clare seemed very distressed. "I'm thirty years old, unemployed and still live at home with my parents. There are only two reasons why I can't get a job. Either there's something wrong with the world or there's something wrong with me. Clearly, the world isn't to blame for where I'm at in life at present, so the problem clearly lies with me. I need fixing. Can you help?"

Wow. I'd only asked her how she was.

Clare had a very black and white view of life – perhaps more so than most of us. But she fell into a trap I believe many of us can fall into.

Believing people can be fixed.

Such people believe there must be a formula. A cure. Some instant solution that will remedy their problem, either with themselves or someone else.

Bite Size Wisdom

> Stop looking for quick fix solutions to complex, long-term problems

Well in case you hadn't noticed, people are not machines. A car or a computer may need a faulty part replacing before it's functioning again, but people are a little more complex. And as soon as you start looking to "fix" people or "fix" yourself you're in trouble.

The problem is we're so used to getting "things" fixed we start believing we can also do the same with people.

The reality is very different.

If you've got trouble with your phone, you can ring a helpline and follow the step-by-step instructions on how to resolve it. Voila. Before you know it your problem is sorted. Carefully follow the instructions on how to erect your flat-pack furniture and before your very eyes emerges your own TV stand with matching set of tables (although to be fair the ones I build end up looking more like a double wardrobe).

But there are no instruction manuals when it comes to dealing with people. Religions may lay out guidelines and principles to live by, but not step-by-step instructions. If there were such a manual it would have to be a very thick one.

Why?

We're complex. We're inconsistent. We react differently to the same event depending on our mood at that particular moment.

When we interact with others there can be a clash of cultures, egos and personalities.

The reality is you cannot treat everybody the same and expect the same outcome. Life, I'm afraid, is just not like that.

Bite Size Wisdom

Avoid the trap of taking a one-size-fits-all approach to dealing with people

So stop looking to fix people. Stop searching for that magical three-point plan that is guaranteed to resolve all your issues. Plenty of writers and speakers promise such solutions.

I believe they're wrong.

Ideas, insights and principles are great.

Suggestions can be helpful.

Techniques may enhance your chances of success.

But let's not kid ourselves that results are guaranteed.

We're dealing with people.

Not motor cars or mobile devices.

So take time to explore lots of ideas in this book that will help you, but let's not fool ourselves that simple solutions exist for everyone's problem.

They don't.

And people cannot be fixed.

Helped? Absolutely.

Encouraged to see things differently? Possibly.

Motivated? Maybe.

Engaged? Perhaps.

Understood more than they currently are? Definitely.

The good news is we can significantly increase our chances of doing all of the above, but never forget this:

Bite Size Wisdom

> You can't control people. But you can do lots to influence them

Oh, and one other thing. They'll never be as straightforward as machines.

Ever.

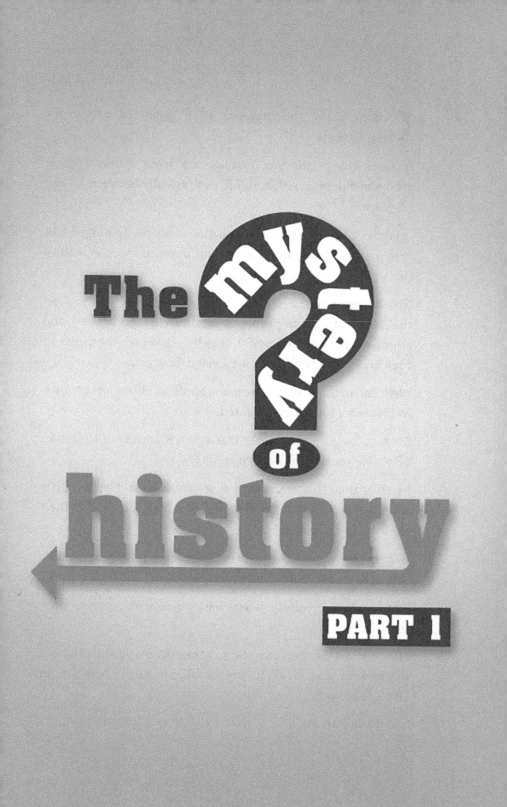

The mystery of history

PART I

Imagine being the manager of a group of people for over 25 years.

Imagine the people you manage are from different backgrounds, different nationalities, and typically between 17 and 35 years old.

Imagine that how you manage these people is judged not just by your boss, but also by millions of people around the world.

Now imagine your every move and decision on how you get the best from these people is monitored meticulously and relentlessly by all aspects of the media – many of whom reckon they know how to do your job better than you.

Welcome to the world of the manager of an elite sports team – in this case, Manchester United.

Sir Alex Ferguson took over managing Manchester United in 1986. He retired 26 years later.

In that time, his team won a staggering 38 trophies. His success was such that the club named a football stand at their stadium in honour of him.

If ever there was a person who knew how to achieve results through people, it was Sir Alex.

That's not an opinion – if you base success on trophies won, it's a fact.

Now I'm aware there may be a rather dramatic shift in your opinion of this book if you dislike football, Manchester United, or both.

But stick with me.

Whatever your attitude towards football or this particular team, let me ask you: how open are you to learn from someone else's success, even if you don't like them?

If you're not open, then feel free to fast forward to the next chapter. But if you are, read on.

I'm fortunate to know someone who worked closely with Sir Alex for over 20 years, the now retired Club Secretary of Manchester United, Ken Merrett. Although never one to put people on a pedestal, and he certainly wouldn't deny that Sir Alex had his flaws, Ken does reveal something fascinating about him.

Sir Alex would never sign a player without having explored their history and background. According to him, the key to signing a good player was not simply about talent, but equally character, and the background they came from.

Clearly, Sir Alex possessed a number of other attributes that led to his and his team's success (and I personally wouldn't be a fan or admirer of all his behaviour), but I was fascinated by his thoroughness in recruiting a player.

Everyone you and I encounter in life has a history. Admittedly, depending on their age, some people's history stretches back further than others, but I've worked with teachers of children under five who would say the background and upbringing of a child, even at a very early age, gives them an insight into the child's behaviour.

In a nutshell, history matters. And the more we're aware of someone's history, the more that can help us understand their current behaviour and give us some clues on how to deal with them.

But we have a challenge.

We're not Sir Alex Ferguson. (And if you think you are, I would strongly recommend you seek out a therapist.)

We don't have many of the privileges he had as a manager. We rarely get to decide who we work with, and few of us will have the necessary financial resources to recruit the very best people for the job. And we might not have the luxury of a support team to help us in our role, or have the option not to work with certain people.

But Ferguson was definitely onto something, which is why I want us to consider "the mystery of history" and to recognize its importance and influence – not just on other people, but also on our own behaviour.

Bite Size Wisdom

History hasn't just shaped other people. It's shaped *you*

Your history has influenced your values, your likes and dislikes, and your perception and understanding of both yourself and others. Depending on your upbringing, it's potentially given you a set of hang-ups, a few hurts, as well as some helpful ways of dealing with life – and in most cases a combination of all three.

Is history always a big deal?

Actually, when it comes to dealing with people, their history is not always a big deal. In fact, in some situations it's irrelevant. My brief encounter with a cashier when I pay for petrol is unlikely to be influenced by either of our past experiences. It could be the first and last time we interact with each other. (OK, the exception to this would be if the petrol station was recently robbed and I walk in wearing a crash helmet.)

But here's the deal.

If you work with someone, if you're dating them, they're a family member, or friend, then being aware of a person's history could be useful in building a better relationship with them.

Bite Size Wisdom

> Being aware of someone's past can help you understand their present

So, what factors play a part in someone's history? Let's explore five of them.

1. Age

I was born in 1964 B.C. (Before Computers[1]). I grew up in a world with three TV channels, all in black and white, which were only available at specific times of the day (i.e. not accessible 24/7), and where one channel, the BBC, ended its coverage every night with the playing of the national anthem. Oh, and the TV we had was rented.

In terms of communication, telephones were attached to a wall, normally alongside a telephone table, and calls were cheaper after 6 p.m. You would never use the phrases "Where have I put my phone?" or "My phone's nearly dead." And if you did, you would get some funny looks.

From a societal standpoint, homosexuality was illegal in the UK, and we still hanged people. The last hangings in the UK took place on the day I was born, 13 August 1964.

As a child, outdoor play was the norm, whatever the weather. If you wanted to stay indoors you either played board games, dressed up in whatever was in the fancy dress box, read a book, or watched the limited amount of television available.

I could go on, but hopefully you get the picture. My children were born in the 1990s and even they grew up in a world vastly different to today. No iPhones. No social media. No online bullying. Trolls were supernatural creatures you read about in children's fairytale books.

The reality is that you and I operate in a world where we interact across four generations: Baby Boomers born between 1942

[1] Yes, I know a few were around in 1964, but they were not commonplace.

and 1965, Generation Xers born between 1966 and 1980, Millennials born between 1981 and 1996, and Gen Zers born between 1997 and 2010. So, although we are all experiencing this moment in time together, depending on our age the worlds we grew up in are vastly different.

Ever really thought about that before?

You see, when you're more aware of the different generations and the vastly different worlds we grew up in, you can appreciate why at times we might not always be on the same wavelength as other people.

It might also explain why some people of the older generation, who may have grown up during the Second World War or been born in its aftermath, may struggle to understand why some people of a younger generation complain about the many challenges of modern life. In many cases, it's just not something they can relate to. The generational differences may also explain some people's attitude of "You've just got to get on with it" as opposed to seeking out the latest wisdom from a self-help guru via a podcast or social media.

Here's another factor from someone's history that may explain the challenges we have dealing with them.

2. Previous experiences

I'm currently working with an organization that's going through a huge amount of change. There's a lot of resistance and negativity to the change from staff. Sound familiar?

So, are this group of people particularly change resistant? Are they more negative than other people in the same situation might be? It would be easy to assume they are. But dig a little bit deeper into the recent history of the organization and the pictures becomes clearer.

This group of people's negativity is actually to do with their previous experiences.

You see, this isn't the first time the organization has gone through some major change. The last time the change programme was sold to the team as *'a series of improvements to increase efficiencies'*. (Don't you love corporate speak?)

In reality, it meant cuts to budgets and staff being made redundant.

You don't have to be Sherlock Holmes to deduce the reasons why this most recent announcement has not been met with shouts of joy and enthusiastically embraced. Is it any surprise that staff have become cynical about management's motives?

Bite Size Wisdom

> A cynic is an idealist who got hurt

The author Rachel Held Evans describes cynicism as calcified anger. If you're dealing with someone who is a cynic, ask yourself why. What's gone on in their past that caused this cynicism? (I'll explore this further in the chapter "Why change is complicated.")

Bite Size Challenge

Think about some of the people you live and work with. Reflect on how their history is affecting how they behave.

The mystery of history

PART 2

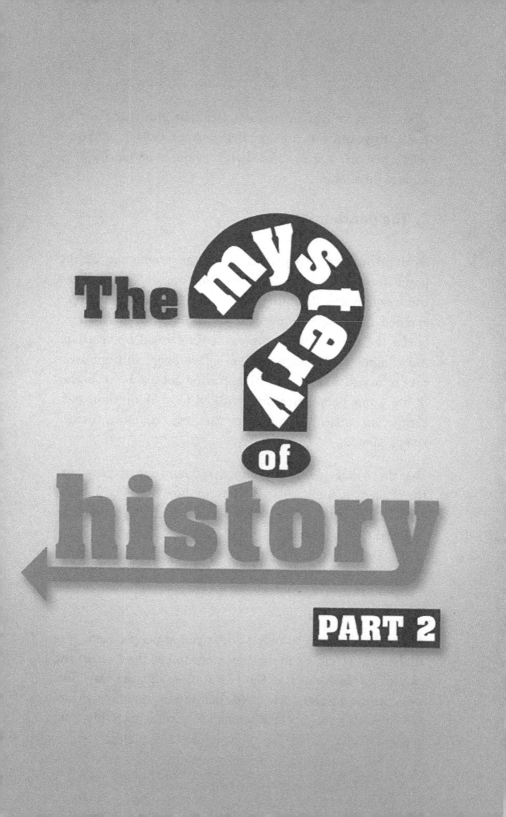

So far, we've explored two factors that influence people's history and can impact their current behaviour. These were a person's age and also their previous experiences. Let's explore three more.

3. The pandemic

During the Covid 19 pandemic a large proportion of the population were required to work from home. Many enjoyed the freedom and flexibility it brought. A number of people avoided the daily commute to and from work and experienced the benefits that the extra time freed up. Perhaps most importantly, the experience gave people an opportunity to reassess their priorities. Having got used to this way of life, some people now feel entitled to work on their own terms, an attitude that was far less common before the pandemic.

That isn't a judgement – it's simply a fact, and one that explains the challenges some organizations are now facing with staff, especially in relation to time spent working from home as opposed to in the office.

As one senior manager said to me recently, "I get the impression staff feel they're doing you a favour by actually coming into work."

And it's also worth thinking about young people who were studying at school or in further education at the time of the pandemic. Not only was their education and the way they were taught severely disrupted, but so was their social life. Whilst some young people seemed to cope remarkably well, others found the adjustment more challenging, and it may be years before we see the full impact of the pandemic on young people's lives. It's worth being mindful of that when we're interacting with them.

4. A previous work culture

You may also encounter people who have worked in a very different work culture than the one they're in now. If some were used to being left to manage their own workload with little day-to-day involvement with their boss, they may struggle within an organization where there's far more interaction with their manager.

My friend Dave talks about the challenges he faced when taking over a team who had previously been led by a manager with an avoidant leadership style, who ducked out of having tough conversations with their team and preferred managing via email rather than face to face. Dave's approach of addressing issues head-on in person was one that came as quite a culture shock to his team.

So, if you're facing challenges with your team, find out how they were previously managed, or what their expectations are about how they're managed. Depending on what they say, you might have to revise those expectations.

5. Upbringing

People's upbringing will influence how they both see and interact with the world. Whilst I know of families whose children have enjoyed international travel and experienced different cultures and traditions from an early age, I've also come across other people who have rarely left the town they were born in, which can give them a very limited perspective on life and lead to them relying on stereotypes of people from other countries and cultures.

Some people you come across on a day-to-day basis have been brought up in an overly protective environment, with the unspoken narrative being that the world is a scary place where it's important to avoid as many risks as possible. Given such an upbringing, it wouldn't come as a shock to discover that these people might struggle with uncertainty and change, and perhaps be less resilient as a result. Agree?

Other people may have experienced a vastly different childhood and been encouraged to explore and take risks, being raised in an environment where bumps and bruises were part of growing up; failing at something was not the end of the world but an opportunity to learn and do better next time.

The reality is, some people you come across inside and outside of work experienced opportunity and encouragement growing up, whereas others experienced instability and an environment devoid of positive emotional support.

Either way, it's hard to deny how such an upbringing has influenced how they are as a person today.

My own upbringing was somewhat chaotic, and I lacked the presence of a father figure for the majority of my childhood.

I was raised almost single-handedly by my mum, and as both my grandfathers died before I was born, I spent large amounts of time with my grandmothers as a child. I think there's been definite upsides to being raised in a predominantly female environment, but I believe I've missed out from not having a male role model in my life.

So, here's something for you to reflect on. (And please do so, even if just for a minute, as the insight could be invaluable.)

How would you describe your own childhood, and how would you say it has shaped who you are today?

That isn't just a question to ask yourself, but perhaps someone else in your personal or professional life. (But probably not the cashier when you're buying petrol.)

What this means for you

It's easy to label people as odd, difficult, or negative. Likewise, we can also label people as happy, great to work with, and full of self-confidence. Whichever it is, just be more mindful that everyone has a backstory. Everyone has a history.

And that backstory and history could be vastly different from yours.

However, this next point is incredibly important.

A person's past is no excuse for inappropriate or unacceptable behaviour in the present – but it could provide clues as to why they behave the way they do.

Bite Size Wisdom

Spend more time being curious about people, and less time judging them

You might want to ponder this question: ***"I wonder what it is about this person's past that's influenced who they are today?"***

Now, clearly understanding and discovering the mystery of history will help build better relationships, but I'm also aware it's unrealistic and, let's be honest, pretty weird, if we were to meet someone and say, ***"Lie down and tell me about your childhood."*** (Which is why I gave up travelling with my inflatable couch years ago.)

If you do try it at work, I think you'll be hearing from HR pretty soon. And asking the question on a first date would either be hilarious or the catalyst for the other person making a hasty exit. (So, if you do want to shorten a date, you now know what to do.)

So, what could help?

The first step is simply increasing your own awareness that everyone's journey is unique to them. You may be a similar age, live in the same town, and even look and sound similar, but believe me you could still be very different. It's worth remembering. . .

Bite Size Wisdom

Differences are not always visible

So, be more mindful and curious about people's pasts – it will give you a window into their present. People's pasts can vary considerably, and whilst someone's history can prepare them to do well in the future, for others it can be the source of pain and the reason for difficult relationships.

In fact, as you read this it might begin to shed light on some of the reasons for your own relationship challenges. However, I do have some good news.

Bite Size Wisdom

A person's past may have helped shape their present, but it doesn't have to determine their destiny

And given my past, that's reassuring to know.

The more you recognize and appreciate your own history as well as other people's, the more likely you are – if you use the ideas in this book – to build a better relationship with them. And you don't have to see a therapist or become a psychiatrist to do so.*

Bite Size Challenge

We've explored five factors from someone's history that can affect how they see and behave in the world. Which of these five has provided the most insight into understanding the people around you? 1. Age. 2. Previous experiences. 3. The pandemic. 4. A previous work culture. 5. Upbringing.

* However, there are occasions when seeing a therapist to help you understand your history could prove invaluable to you.

Most
people
suffer from
S.A.D.S.

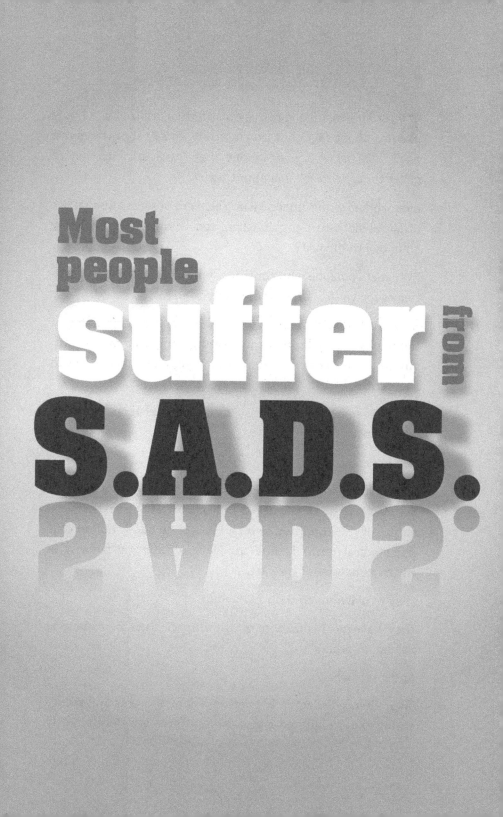

Ever known anyone for years and then realized you know lots about them but they actually know very little about you? Ever asked anyone about their weekend but they've never thought to ask you about yours?

Ever worked with someone who seems to possess a similar set of social skills to Genghis Khan and who seems completely oblivious to the fact?

Ever met someone who continually finishes off your . . . sentences for you . . . often incorrectly?

Ever worked with someone who has an annoying habit of talking over people in team meetings and who you're convinced has never really listened to anyone but themselves in their entire life?

Ever met someone who seems very insightful about everyone but themselves?

You have?

Then you've probably met someone suffering from S.A.D.S. **S**elf-**A**wareness **D**eficiency **S**yndrome. Of course the very nature of this condition (which I hasten to add is not an official medical term) means the person suffering from it is entirely unaware of the fact.

They're oblivious to their behaviour.

They have no realization of the impact their behaviour is having on others.

And guess what?

Their chances of actually reading a book like this and recognizing they might be a S.A.D.S. sufferer are only slightly above zero. And even if by some remote chance they did find themselves reading this book (presumably because their manager, friend or partner bought it for them) it's still highly unlikely they would recognize themselves in this section.

Which, ironically, is in itself one of the main symptoms of S.A.D.S.

And as you're reading this section you're probably thinking of people in your world who suffer from it, aren't you?

But before you sit back and relax into your armchair of smugness beware of the following.

You yourself may be prone to bouts of S.A.D.S.

To some degree at least.

Now before you start protesting at such an unfounded accusation, recognize that all of us have our blind spots.

Yes even you. And me. (And I'm the one who came up with the term!)

Now some people are definitely more self-aware than others.

The nature of certain jobs like counselling, teaching and nursing encourages people to self-reflect. And I recognize many other professions will do too.

In some organizations I've worked with, to encourage self-reflection and increase self-awareness managers not only give their staff feedback but the staff also give feedback to their managers. That isn't always a comfortable experience but it does help people to gain an insight into their behaviour and how they're perceived by others.

It's also not an exercise that's designed solely to point out people's faults but to provide a balanced perspective on how others see you, which will include highlighting many of your positive traits that you may take for granted.

And all of the above can help us be less prone to S.A.D.S. However, the following piece of wisdom is one to reflect on and chew over:

Bite Size Wisdom

> Rarely do we truly see ourselves as others see us

Now like with many illnesses there's a spectrum in terms of the severity of S.A.D.S. In extreme cases there may even be a medical reason for people's seemingly gross lack of interpersonal skills and self-awareness such as some forms of autism (which in certain cases may be undiagnosed).

But all of us can from time to time suffer from S.A.D.S., even if only mildly.

Now you may believe you're more self-aware than most people you know, and even taking the time to reflect on the question "How self-aware am I?" would be a good indication of that fact. So too would be taking the time to read this book.

They're all positive signs, but they don't guarantee that you have high levels of self-awareness and that you truly understand yourself and your impact on others.

You may actually fall into the trap of devouring this kind of material and believe acquiring knowledge is the key to you succeeding with people.

It isn't.

It's what you do with what you know that counts.

Knowledge only takes you so far. It's when you decide to start doing something, or perhaps just as importantly stop doing something, that you begin to see the fruit of that knowledge.

So recognize that although you may encounter people who clearly are suffering from a strong case of S.A.D.S. we can all experience mild symptoms.

This insight will help you understand why some people you encounter will be very difficult to deal with but it will also keep you humble enough to recognize that none of us are immune from it and that we all need help to improve from where we are now.

One final important point to make before ending this chapter. Some people's behaviour could stem from their neurodiversity – in other words, their brain affects how they experience and engage with the world, and therefore the people within it.

Although applied to a range of people, the term neurodiversity is often used in the context of Autism Spectrum Disorder (ASD). So don't automatically assume that someone's behaviour is rooted in their lack of self-awareness; it could actually be rooted in their neurobiology.

Bite Size Challenge

1. When was the last time you asked someone close to you to give you their perspective on how you come across to them and others?
2. Ask six people in your life to come up with 10 words to describe you. Reflect on those words and see if there are any surprises or ones you wish weren't there. Then ask for more feedback on why they came up with those words, and any suggestions they might have to help you accentuate the positive aspects of your character and reduce the less positive ones. (Remember though, you're working with people's perceptions of you, which could be influenced by all kinds of factors. So look for common themes in the feedback you receive.)

Some people are lightbulbs

I trained to be a probation officer as part of my degree. People and how they behave fascinate me. But having studied for four years I decided not to pursue it as a career.

There were lots of reasons for my decision. But during interviews for other types of jobs I didn't want to get bogged down in explaining these reasons why. I had already fallen into that trap previously, where my interview focused more on the reasons why people commit crime and why I didn't feel cut out to work with such people rather than the job I was actually applying for.

So I implemented a cunning plan that dealt with the question as to why I didn't want to be a probation officer speedily and succinctly.

It went as follows:

Interviewer: So why didn't you want to pursue a career as a probation officer?

Me: Well to put a slight twist on an old joke, "How many probation officers does it take to change a lightbulb? One. But only if the lightbulb wants to change."

Now I suspect as you're reading the above you are not currently doubled up in laughter and wondering why I don't have my own comedy show. I'm wise enough to know that the world of comedy is not about to be turned upside down with my sudden appearance onto the scene.

But here's my point.

Whether it was due to stunned amazement that I had said something so unfunny or the fact they felt I had said something deeply profound and therefore didn't want to appear stupid, most interviewers smiled (well slightly) and moved on to their next question.

My cunning plan had worked.

Result.

And the reason for the above anecdote?

Well, there are actually some people in life who are lightbulbs.

They refuse to change.

And if you really want to succeed with people then don't waste vast amounts of time and energy trying to change people who don't want to change.

By all means try. For a while.

But be careful.

Bite Size Wisdom

> Don't delude yourself into thinking that you can automatically succeed where everyone else has failed

To put it bluntly, when it comes to dealing with some people, rearrange into a well-known phrase or saying:

"Brick wall banging like head your against a."

So why might someone behave like a lightbulb and not want to change?

Here are two reasons:

i. They want to stand out from the crowd. They like to appear different from everyone else and always take the opposite viewpoint. This is not done for genuine reasons but because it meets their need for attention and sense of self-importance. They might actually enjoy winding others up. Do you know anyone like that? Remember this: people behave in a way that gets their needs met.

Bite Size Wisdom

> We all need to feel important – it's just that some people damage their relationships in their desire to achieve it

ii. Some people have a very fixed view about the world and life in general. They know what they believe and what is right and what is wrong. And there can be a real sense of safety and security in this belief. It's comfortable. The last thing they want is for this to be challenged or for their world to be rocked.

So why be open to change? Why explore other possibilities? Why make myself feel uncomfortable?

Far safer to stand firm. Resist. Be cynical.

You see, it takes courage to change at times. It takes humility to admit you may be wrong. And some people are simply not courageous or humble enough to do so.

Harsh?

Perhaps. But it may well explain why some people remain lightbulbs.

Bite Size Wisdom

> Remember, people's stubbornness is a choice. It's not a medical condition

But there is some good news. People don't have to remain a "lightbulb." They can change. But here's the key: only if *they* want to. Remember, they'll do so for *their* reasons, not yours. And perhaps only if they're helped to do so.

It's possible that some people's "lightbulb" behaviour is only temporary. So meeting their need to feel important and providing plenty of support in times of change can help. So too can admitting your own struggle with change at times. Make sure you look out for ideas in the rest of this book that might help switch them on, especially in the chapter "How to make change a success" in Section Two. You see, it's possible that you've been flicking the wrong switch so far, but what you're about to read might help you find the right one.

Bite Size Challenge

How fixed in your outlook would you say you are? How easy do you find it to change your mind or opinion about someone? Can you think of an example where you have changed your viewpoint about a person or situation?

Why intelligent people do stupid things

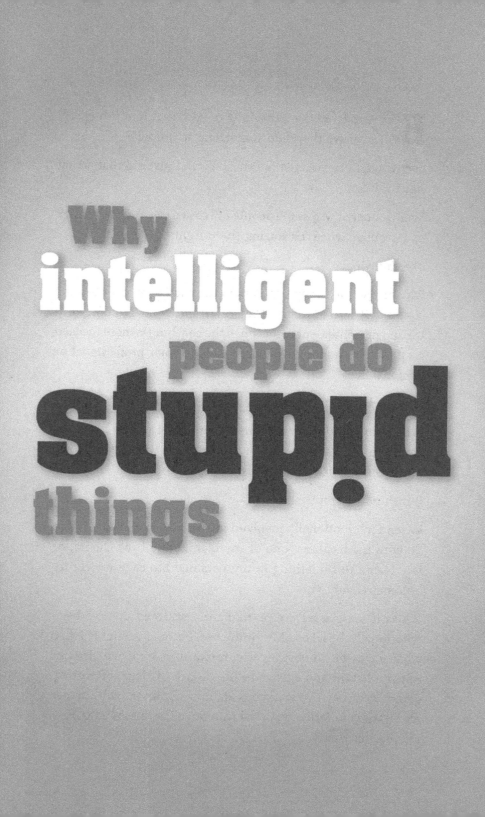

Ever witnessed the behaviour of someone and thought "I can't believe they'd do something so stupid"?

Ever thought to yourself "I can't believe I just did that. What was I thinking?"

Ever wondered why some people fail to see the obvious answer to a problem when it's staring them right in the face?

I certainly have.

Part of my role in my business is to coach people. Often the coaching is related to how they can improve as a communicator and presenter, but sometimes the coaching is more focused on particular issues people are facing in their professional or personal lives.

Here's what's interesting.

When I'm emotionally detached from the situation I find my ability to see the cause of the problem and the possible solutions comes quickly and easily.

But there's a problem.

When I'm emotionally involved in the situation, when it's to do with my business, one of my team, one of my clients, or it's related to something in my personal life then my clarity becomes cloudy.

It's as if my glasses are permanently steamed up. I've been emotionally hijacked. My brain can become scrambled and what might be an obvious way forward to someone else can remain distant and elusive to me. A lack of sleep, often triggered because we're worrying about a situation, will further exacerbate our lack of rational thinking. Tiredness can trigger terrible decisions.

That's why seemingly rational, intelligent, successful people do stupid things and often miss the obvious.

So when we're closely involved in a situation or physically and emotionally tired, our rational perspective often takes a back seat. And in its place steps up our emotional brain, which takes a firm grip of the controls of our decision making. Sometimes with dire consequences.

Bite Size Wisdom

> Your emotions can cloud the view to your solutions

That's why at times it's absolutely critical that you *don't* strike whilst the iron is hot. Because when you do there's a strong chance that someone is going to get burnt. (You may just want to re-read that last point again. It could save you a lot of heartache in the future.)

Remember, when you're feeling either "mad," "bad" or "sad" you're not thinking straight. And often when we're in an emotional state we look for a short-term solution to a long-term problem. Our brains drive us to act, not think.

So what does this look like in reality?

Parents can lash out with totally inappropriate and disproportionate punishments for their children. "You're grounded for three months."

Managers speak first and think later, "I never want him near this building again."

Customers can wildly overreact to a minor issue and go to extraordinary and time-consuming lengths to argue their case.

If any of this seems familiar to you then welcome to dealing with the human race. It's not easy, is it?

So don't be deceived by our technological advances and our sophisticated ways of living. Deep down we still show remarkable similarities to our evolutionary ancestors.

Bite Size Wisdom

> Our ways of communication may have evolved, but sometimes our ways of thinking haven't

So please, never ever assume that logic is running the show. It isn't.

And it's not just something other people are prone to. You're prone to this form of illogical and irrational thinking and behaviour as well. Drugs and alcohol will exacerbate our "stupidness," but so too will increased stress.

I'm really not exaggerating when I say *"stress makes you stupid."*

And conversely so too can feelings of high elation that can lead us into making rash promises and rash decisions whilst we're still caught up on an emotional high. Despite our later regrets our pride can kick in and make us feel compelled to stick with these promises and decisions. We can convince ourselves that to change our mind might appear foolish. Yet the reality is not changing your mind and admitting you may have acted rashly is stupid. But that's the danger when we allow our emotions to completely hijack our decisions.

Bite Size Wisdom

> Never underestimate intelligent people's ability to make really stupid decisions

So as you read on look for ideas to manage your emotions more effectively and by doing so be more effective and less reactive in dealing with people.

Bite Size Challenge

If you've already overreacted to a situation or a person what will you do to ensure a better outcome next time?

You get what you tolerate

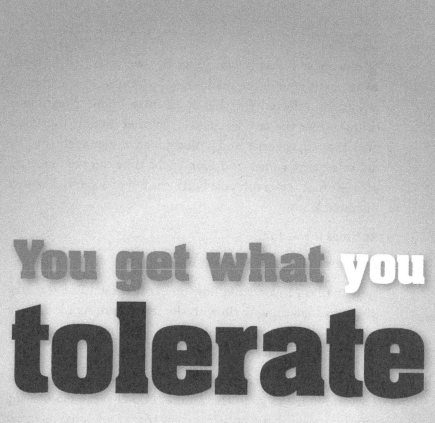

I remember years ago going on a two-week residential management course for graduates. I was one of the chosen few to be selected for this apparently highly prestigious course. Over the two weeks we explored models (business ones that is), theories and philosophies of management. We did role plays, games and even spent time outside jumping off a 40-foot telegraph pole (with the aid of a safety harness of course).

At times it was fun.

At times I felt completely out of my depth.

And at times I wondered how on earth what I was learning about had anything to do with the real world. As I look back on the experience I remember only one thing. Jumping off that telegraph pole.

I certainly don't recall any advice or pearls of wisdom that have stood me in good stead since. I don't recall discovering anything new about myself, except that if you give me a set of business accounts to read I might as well be looking at an ancient long lost Hebrew manuscript.

I didn't feel equipped in any way, shape or form to advance my management career. It was so disappointing to spend two weeks on a course and to have so very little to show for it. In my opinion it was a complete waste of the company's money and my time.

I wonder if you've ever had a similar experience? I hope not.

Now let's fast forward a few years from then. Despite my previous experience I was still keen to invest in my development and decided to attend a one-day seminar in the UK, run by an American company called CareerTrack. For a relatively small sum of money you could turn up for a day and explore topics such as "How to deliver exceptional customer service" and "How to discipline employees and correct performance problems." (Sexy title, eh? Bet you wish you'd been to that one don't you?)

I, along with a hundred or so other business people, were sitting in a hotel conference room listening to some American guy enthusiastically telling us about his family and which part of the US he was from. I remember thinking that if things didn't improve at least I'd only wasted a day of my time, not two weeks.

And then it happened.

Almost casually the speaker Harry Chambers remarked, "You may want to write down this next bit. If you're managing people I think you'll probably find it useful."

Then Harry gave us two statements. It's nearly 30 years since I attended the event but I've never forgotten them. They've become engraved into my memory. I hope they become engraved in yours too. Because if they do I believe they will influence how you deal with people.

Ready for them?

OK. Here goes.

> **"We receive the performance (or behaviour) we are willing to tolerate."**

and

> **"My silence, denial or avoidance gives approval to the situation."**

Simple statements.

But very powerful.

No complex management theories to wrestle with or in-depth questionnaires to fill in. In fact I guess it probably only took me a couple of minutes to write them down. And yet I've been pondering them ever since.

In hindsight I realize they're obvious statements really. But we don't always see the obvious do we? So let's unpack each statement a little and see how they relate to our day-to-day lives.

Let's start with the first one: "We receive the performance (or behaviour) we are willing to tolerate."

If you tolerate people being continually late without there ever being any consequences, guess what will continue to happen?

Tolerate someone continually putting you down and that behaviour will continue.

Tolerate people underperforming in your team and they'll see no reason to change.

Tolerate poor service and that's what you'll continue to receive.

Tolerate the behaviour of a loved one even though it hurts you and the cycle will continue.

Here's the deal. Plain and simple.

Bite Size Wisdom

> You get what you tolerate. Problems persist because we get used to them

The question is, are you happy with what you're currently tolerating? Or do you just simply moan about it but continue to accept it?

Right, now onto that second statement: "My silence, denial or avoidance gives approval to the situation." Let's chew over that one for a moment.

In a nutshell, the reality is your non-actions still have an impact. Doing nothing is still doing something.

Challenging stuff, eh?

Bite Size Wisdom

> Your silence is still saying something

So are you comfortable with the messages you're sending to others by saying and doing nothing? Are you relaxed about how others might see and treat you as a result?

If you are, fine.

That's your choice.

But please don't continue to moan, complain and resent someone (or some organization) if the only thing you're prepared to do is . . .

absolutely nothing.

Bite Size Wisdom

> No matter how much you want them to be, people are not mind readers

People sometimes behave in a state of blissful ignorance, oblivious and unaware of the impact of their behaviour on you and others. And that's unlikely to change if you say and do nothing.

But please hear me right. I'm not suggesting people will immediately change if you do confront their behaviour (and as we'll see later, there are effective and less effective ways to go about this) but at least it's a start. At least the issue is out in the open. Things might get messy, but at least the boil has been lanced and there's an opportunity to deal with what was hidden beneath the surface. An added bonus is it can provide an outlet for the potential anger and resentment that was possibly building up within you.

When you stop tolerating and start talking you lay down the path towards a better and potentially more positive relationship. And by doing so you're more likely to succeed in dealing with people.

Bite Size Challenge

Is there someone's behaviour you've tolerated for too long? Are you prepared to live with the consequences or is it time to challenge them?

Why change is complicated

Benjamin Franklin was many things in life, but lazy wasn't one of them. He lived in the 1700s and, amongst many other things, was a writer, inventor, scientist, and one of the Founding Fathers of the United States.

Amazing what people did with their time before social media, Netflix, and free WiFi.

He's often credited with the following quote:

> *"In this world nothing can be said to be certain, except death and taxes."*

If he was alive today, I think he would add a third. Change.

Do we really hate change?

There's a common, widely held belief that people don't like change.

Really?

Still travelling to work by horse and using your Nokia mobile phone? (If you are, please be careful not to text and ride.)

The fact is, we're actually quite comfortable with change when. . .

- It's our choice
- We're in control
- We see the benefits of changing
- We see the downsides of not changing

Starting a family, moving house, booking a holiday somewhere new, or buying a pet are all examples of when people not only don't resist change, but actually instigate it.

Even when we're not the creators of change, we can still end up embracing it.

Your world and mine changed dramatically in March 2020 with the global pandemic. I made a living from speaking at events – my world centred around being in a room with other people. My business was decimated, and I appreciate this was nothing in comparison with the devastating impact the pandemic had on many people's lives.

After a few weeks I realized the world wasn't going to return to normal any time soon. If my business was going to survive I would need to change and start delivering virtual events. And I had zero experience in doing so. I lacked the expertise, the equipment (who knew lighting was such a big deal?) and, if I'm honest, the confidence. But here's why the dramatic change to how I worked was not that scary.

Firstly, although the change took some adjusting to, ultimately it was my choice, and I was in control of how many events I did and the way I chose to deliver them. (I decided to avoid sharing slides and went old school, using a flipchart instead. I used props, made the sessions interactive using the chat box, and actually grew to really enjoy delivering them.)

I also saw the benefit of changing. My material could help a lot of people, particularly at such a challenging time and, let's be blunt about it, I realized the consequence of not changing: a dramatic loss of income.

Added to that, my work gave me a real sense of purpose and a connection with the outside world. And I genuinely believe not embracing change would have had a hugely detrimental effect on my well-being.

Over a two-and-a-half-year period I delivered over 200 virtual events, literally around the world: from Melbourne to Manchester and from Sri Lanka to Iran. All from the cosy confines of my home office in North West England.

Changing wasn't easy, believe me. Mastering technology was a challenge for me (just ask my wife), but those four factors (choice, control, seeing the benefits of change, and seeing the downsides of not changing) all helped chip away at my previous Luddite approach to technology.

Which is just as well, because. . .

Bite Size Wisdom

> The most insecure place to be right now is in an organization that's not changing

Why is change a challenge to people?

OK, so we might not actually hate change as much as we're sometimes led to believe but, let's be honest, it can still be very challenging. Agree?

And clearly that's the case when it's not our choice, we're not in control, we don't see any benefit for ourselves, and fail to see the downsides of not changing.

You see, when it comes to the whole subject of change we experience the following paradox:

Bite Size Wisdom

> People have a love/
> hate relationship
> with change

And that's why change is complicated.

OK, so having looked at some factors for why people can be comfortable with change, let's take some time to reflect on the reasons why you and the people you live and work with sometimes also resist it.

Five reasons for resistance

1. Change can be seen as a threat.

You and I have something in common with each other – our brains enjoy predictability and certainty. Admittedly not all the time – life would become incredibly boring if that was the case – but in order to function well, predictability and a sense of certainty around many aspects of our lives is important to us as human beings. And although the unknown can be exciting (especially when it's your choice to explore it) it's less appealing when it's thrust upon you.

Now although there is a small percentage of the population who constantly seek out new adventures and could be labeled "adrenaline addicts" (I have a close family member who could fall into this category), generally we all like to feel safe and secure, and we benefit from routines and rituals – including those lovers of the adrenaline rush.

In a nutshell, routines and rituals help us relax, and although we want to avoid getting into a rut, the reality is. . .

Bite Size Wisdom

Constant uncertainty
and unpredictability
amplify our anxiety

So, whilst the prospect of change could create opportunities for some people, it could also be a threat to the safe, predictable and comfortable worlds of others.

2. Change can lead to a loss of status.

We all gain a sense of self-worth from our abilities and achievements. It feels good to be good at something and to be recognized for that fact. There's nothing wrong with that. As a species we are status-driven. It might seem incredibly shallow to say so, but our perceived status affects how people treat us.

Why is that the case?

Well, according to Will Storr, author of the bestselling book *The Status Game*, it seems to be a product of our evolution. A perceived higher status of our early ancestors is believed to have meant they got access to better mates, more food, and greater safety for themselves and their offspring. In other words, status was inextricably linked to survival and having more sex.

Luxury brands have a lot to thank our ancient hunter-gatherer ancestors for.

Perceived status can be achieved in many ways – through what you wear, the car you drive, and the people you hang around with.

And here's where it can play a part in influencing some people's response to change.

You see, status can also be achieved through your knowledge and expertise and your position within an organization (which goes a long way to explaining some people's love of fancy job titles).

But what if a particular change (perhaps as a result of AI) means the skills you possessed to reach a certain position or status in life are no longer necessary – that they're now redundant? Or what about if a particular change means you need the support of someone you perceive as junior to yourself?

Potentially that's a threat to both your esteem and your employability. When you're no longer perceived as the top dog with all the privileges that go with that position and you've seen your status slide, it's unlikely you'll be at the front of the queue enthusiastically embracing the new change.

3. Change can lead to a loss of control.

People don't like to be micro-managed. That might be a requirement when you're a toddler, but even at an early age you begin to see the signs of children wanting to assert their own independence (which may explain the outfits my daughter wore when she was three).

That's even more the case as adults.

Bite Size Wisdom

Although some people are more compliant than others, deep down there's an inner rebel within all of us

Admittedly, the size of that rebel differs from person to person (if you've got children, you will probably relate to this), and adolescence and alcohol often act as a catalyst to unleash it, but none of us enjoy being constantly told what to do. (Ever seen a sign that says "DO NOT TOUCH" and then felt a strong urge to do so?)

That's why when we feel change is being imposed on us, without any influence or input from ourselves, we can feel a greater desire to kick back against it.

4. A poor relationship with those implementing the change.

Some change is resisted not because of the actual change, but because of who's instigated it.

Bite Size Wisdom

If you don't like a person, it's unlikely you'll like their ideas

If you don't respect those who are implementing the change, your resistance is ramped up. Your inner rebel is awakened. Let's face it, it takes a degree of maturity and humility to admit, "I might not like that person, but I agree with their ideas."

Resistance in these cases is driven primarily by emotion, not logic. The reality is the change could actually be beneficial to you, but you could adamantly refuse to embrace it because of the person or people who've initiated it.

Ever had that experience, or come across someone who acted that way?

5. Previous experiences of change.

I was chatting to my friend Chris recently, who told me how her new boss was enthusiastically championing the latest changes in her school. The problem was, Chris had been in her role longer than her boss, and the latest initiative was actually an old idea, but given a new label.

Sound familiar?

Chris was also aware that this "new initiative" had failed to achieve its previous aims and been abandoned and replaced with something else. Now, years later, the corpse of the idea was being resurrected.

Chris is a passionate, positive person, who's not prone to pessimism, but even she found it hard to keep her cynicism in check. To use another analogy, the packaging might have changed, but the product was still the same.

I've seen so many organizations where changes are announced with great fanfare, but people who have worked with their organization for a long time have seen previous initiatives fade and fizzle out until the latest new way of working is introduced with an even greater array of bells and whistles.

Perhaps some "old timers" are not being cynical because they don't like change, but because of their experience of previous changes that didn't work. This can especially be the case when the idea for the change was made by people who are removed from the day-to-day impact of it and fail to appreciate the consequences it can lead to in people's lives.

Bite Size Wisdom

> Cynicism is often fueled by the broken promises of the past and the stupid decisions of the present

That's why this next point is crucial. Rather than blame people for their cynicism, it would be a far more effective approach to try and understand the reasons for it in the first place. And if the cynicism is misplaced, there's an opportunity to counter it before it spreads.

Here's a recap of the five reasons why people might resist change:

1. Change is seen as a threat
2. Change can lead to a loss of status
3. Change can lead to a loss of control
4. A poor relationship with those implementing the change
5. Previous experiences of change

So when it comes to dealing with people in times of change, it's complicated. Sometimes it is enthusiastically embraced, whilst other times it's stubbornly resisted. This chapter has been about helping you understand the reasons behind people's reactions. If you want to know how best to support people in times of change, check out the chapter "How to make change a success" coming up later in the book.

Bite Size Challenge

Think about some of the changes you've been experiencing in your world. How have you responded? What has caused you to respond the way you have? Review the five reasons why people resist change. Which of them could be the reasons why the people you live or work with are resisting change?

Humiliation is for amateurs

Three young managers accosted me at the end of one of my business presentations. They had a problem with one of their team called Barry. Apparently, he was their most difficult and awkward employee. In their years of managing him they informed me they'd tried everything to turn around his performance and attitude. They hoped a brief explanation of their challenge with Barry would extract from me a pearl of wisdom or golden nugget that would immediately transform his performance overnight.

It's fair to say their expectations of me were hugely unrealistic, although not entirely uncommon. Some people seem to think that because I write books and speak at conferences, this somehow transforms me into some mystical guru who is able to reveal ancient ideas and wisdom which until that point had remained hidden from humankind.

Sadly I'm not.

Which is a pity really, because in some ways I could get quite used to the idea.

However, armed with these false hopes and a problem employee my three managers put me firmly on the spot.

"So, what do you think we should do with Barry then, Paul?"

I tried to look guru-like and also buy some time, so I answered their question with a question.

"What's been your approach with Barry so far?"

"Well, we've tried the obvious."

"The obvious?" I enquired.

"Well yeah, we've tried humiliation."

Although struggling to quite comprehend what I'd just heard I somehow managed to mumble another question and maintain my guru-like persona.

"And how did that go down?"

"Well, to be fair, Paul, it just seemed to make Barry worse."

"Really, you don't say" I said, trying to contain my amazement at what was clearly an entirely inappropriate and ineffective approach.

But our conversation got me thinking. Why on earth would they think that humiliating someone was an obvious approach?

Maybe these three managers were only copying their role models. Perhaps a parent, teacher or even their own manager had tried this strategy with them previously. Maybe they'd witnessed humiliation being used as a tactic on others.

Whatever their reasons, let's be clear. When it comes to dealing with people, humiliation is the hallmark of a malevolent dictator, a sign of someone who has their own self-esteem issues or an indication of a complete lack of knowledge and experience in dealing with others.

Bite Size Wisdom

Humiliating someone is not an indication of your strength. It's a reflection of your weakness

It's like crushing a nut with a chieftain tank. Unhelpful, unnecessary, and wholly destructive.

It's the same with people. Deliberately humiliating someone is not a form of motivation, but it is laying down the foundation for bitterness, resentment and perhaps even revenge in the future.

The last football match I attended with my late father was way back in 2008. It's a game I'll never forget – not because of what happened during the game, but what happened at half time. Let me explain.

It was December 2008 and Phil Brown, the manager of Hull City at the time, found his team 4–0 down at half time, away from home to Manchester City. So, angered by his team's first half performance, Brown decided to conduct his half-time team talk on the pitch in front of the travelling Hull City fans. Players subsequently described being lectured by their manager in front of their own fans as a humiliating experience.

So what was the impact?

Up until that game, Hull City's record was Played 18 Won 7 Drew 5 Lost 6 – a total of 26 points. In their next 20 matches Hull City went on to win only 1 more game, losing 14 and drawing 5. That's just 8 points.

They survived relegation by a single point.

Some people do feel humiliated by their own performance, or because of a mistake they've made. In these cases, it can make them determined to never face such an experience again. But this form of humiliation is self-inflicted. It's not the same as being humiliated by someone else.

Now if you do have to give someone some challenging feedback, please remember this: ***Where you say it and who's present when you say it can be just as important as the actual words you use.***

Having worked in the Far East I'm aware of the importance in the Asian culture of "saving face." In other words, do all you can to ensure another person retains their self-respect, especially in front of others.

But let's not dismiss this as not being an important factor in Western culture also.

Here's the reality.

No one likes to look stupid, no matter what country they live in. A fundamental human need is a desire to feel competent, useful and valued.

So if you want to influence and engage people and switch them on to your way of thinking, then take humiliation for a hike.

Bite Size Wisdom

Only clowns are
happy to look stupid

If you have something to say that is potentially negative or critical, consider the following points:

- Will I still want to say this in 24 hours?
- What's my end goal in saying what I'm about to say?

- Am I aware of the long-term effect my words may have on this person?
- Where am I best saying what I have to say?
- Who else, if anyone, needs to be there when I say it?

Some people are more naturally resilient than others. Perhaps they have thicker skin and can quickly brush off criticism. It washes over them. But humiliation is more than criticism. It strikes at the heart of a person's self-esteem. It wounds their pride. It attacks the core of their identity.

Being humiliated could literally crush some people psychologically, particularly if they're already demoralized and less thick skinned. And if the person on the receiving end of the humiliation is a child and the perpetrator is a parent the damage can be long lasting.

So make sure you check out the chapter "How to make criticism count, not crucify," and challenge your own motives behind what you're saying. Be honest, is it to help or hurt the other person?

To make sure your communication is seen as less of a personal attack, and in order to soften the blow, if you have something to say try a couple of the following ideas.

Firstly, when you disagree with someone you could ask "Do you mind if I play devil's advocate for a moment?" That way it's as if you've introduced another character into the conversation. You're actually gaining the other person's permission to challenge their ideas, not by doing so as yourself, but in your role as devil's advocate. It becomes far easier to challenge someone when you're "playing" this role and it de-personalizes what you're saying.

Secondly, remember people find it easier (not easy, but easier) and less painful to hear negative news from their mouth than from someone else's. So rather than telling people directly what you thought simply ask:

> *"What've you learned from that experience?"*

followed by

> *"If you had a chance to do that again, what would you do differently?"*

Now if they say "nothing" then you've got a bigger problem than you realized. Not only is this person incompetent, they're also oblivious to the fact! (And probably suffering from S.A.D.S. – see the chapter "Most people suffer from S.A.D.S.") To be honest this is rare, and asking such questions gives the other person time to reflect and hopefully come up with their learning and a better approach next time. As they've now started going down this track it also makes it easier for you to build on their thoughts and ideas and offer some of your own. This will feel to the other person like they're in a conversation with you rather than being criticized by you.

Finally another strategy that I've found hugely helpful in addressing a challenging and perhaps awkward situation whilst allowing the other person to save face is to ask them this question:

> *"If you were me what would you do?"*

This again gives someone the opportunity to come up with their own ideas for a way forward and although you might not necessarily agree with them entirely, they're being treated more like an adult rather than a naughty child.

Make sure you take the above seriously.

Bite Size Wisdom

> From children through to colleagues, the pain of being humiliated can have long-term negative consequences not just for them, but for you also

People may need to be challenged. They may need a wake-up call. But they do not need to be humiliated. Ever.

Bite Size Challenge

Which of these three strategies, "playing devil's advocate," asking "what've you learned and what would you do differently?" and "if you were me what would you do?" will you use to help rather than potentially humiliate someone?

Being nice won't always work

There's a huge myth around dealing with people that states you should always be nice to them. Whilst I'm not advocating you be nasty I am suggesting that one of the reasons you could be failing with people is because you're actually too nice.

Let me explain.

I was talking to a woman who was bemoaning her new female boss's recent arrival at the store where she worked. Morale had plummeted and I immediately leapt to the conclusion that this was due to the manager's inability to motivate and deal with her staff.

I was wrong. Well, to a degree anyway.

The staff were demotivated, but not for the reasons you would expect.

Their new boss was a great one for professional standards. She questioned why people were late getting to work or late back from breaks. She expected hard work from her employees and held regular team meetings.

This came as quite a shock in comparison with the previous manager's style of management, which at best could be described as "laid back and easy going."

Staff were not happy. Some had been used to ringing in sick on a Saturday morning after a heavy night out on Friday. Whilst the previous manager accepted they "had a bit of a cold" and told them not to worry, their new boss was less accommodating. Whilst not accusing them of lying, she seemed low on sympathy and high on making them aware of the consequences their absence was having on the rest of the team. Apparently things were now so bad some staff were contemplating leaving as they sought an easier ride somewhere else.

Their previous manager may well have been described as "nice." They were certainly popular. But the store was underperforming. The staff were exploiting the manager's relaxed and non-confrontational style.

Bite Size Wisdom

> If your main goal in life is to be popular, go and sell ice cream

Here's the deal.

If you want to make a positive difference in life you need to recognize that means you're not always going to be liked by everyone. At times, just like the manager in the above example, you will be disliked. And that's OK. As the author Robin Sharma says:

Bite Size Wisdom

> People with a need to be liked don't change the world

Powerful stuff, eh?

Being too nice can also send mixed and unclear messages to others.

Let me explain.

Sometimes when nice people are pushed to a point where even they need to say something about someone's behaviour their message can still be lost in a sea of "diplomatic let's not cause offence waffle." Here's what I mean. I'll exaggerate the point to make the point:

> *"Hi, sorry to be a pain. I just wondered if at some stage when it's convenient, if it's not too much trouble, would it be OK if, and there's no rush, but would it be possible, when it works for you, if you wouldn't mind taking your foot off my neck. Thanks. I really do appreciate it."*

The reality is people can exploit your niceness as a weakness. You're not succeeding with people with this approach.

You're failing.

OK there may be some perceived superficial benefits with such an approach. People may speak well of you. You may be popular. Even well liked. But are you succeeding? Really?

Bite Size Wisdom

To be successful with people it's more important to be respected than to be liked

You may of course have built up such a good relationship with people that you're respected and liked. Great. Wonderful. But if I had to choose which is the most important of the two I'd go for respect.

Now please don't go out of your way to be nasty. But if an underperforming team member sees you as less of a soft touch, and that challenging neighbour or awkward friend has decided to back down a little, then perhaps you're discovering the benefits of not being too nice. You don't have to ditch your diplomacy to do so, but you do need to ditch the need to always be liked.

Bite Size Challenge

Has your niceness ever been exploited by others? Have you learnt from the experience? Is there a situation now where your "niceness" is actually damaging the relationship?

It takes two to tango

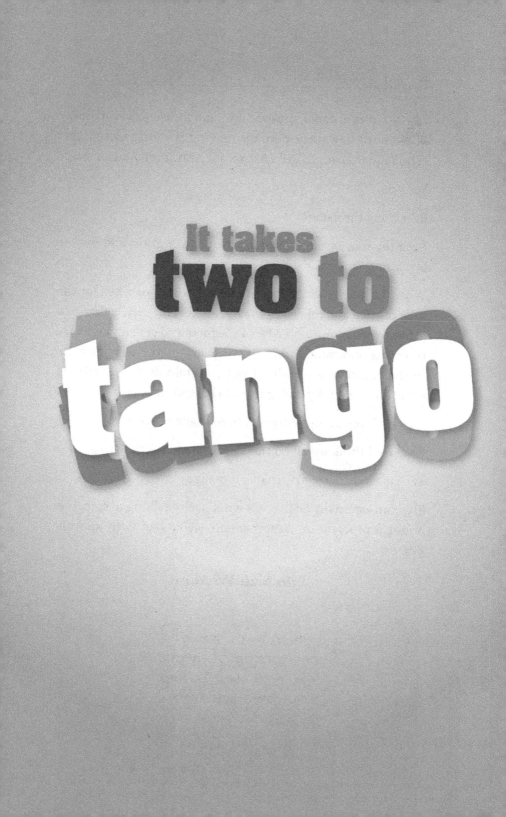

As a professional speaker I'm sometimes asked if I ever embellish a story, perhaps making it a little more interesting and amusing than it was in reality. And my honest answer?

Yes I do.

Ever done the same?

I see my role as a speaker as not only to inform and inspire but also to entertain.

When I'm telling a story there are also occasions when for the sake of time and relevance I miss out certain details. My goal is not to communicate 100% of the facts and give my audience too much information but to get over a particular point. As to the question of whether I put a certain degree of spin on what I'm saying, I plead guilty as charged.

So what's my point? Why is this relevant to you?

Because I think we all do the same.

Perhaps more regularly than we realize.

This can especially be the case when we're talking to someone about a problem or disagreement we've had with another person.

Bite Size Wisdom

Whenever we tell our version of events we instantly become our own personal spin doctor

Very often when we begin to recount a particular event or incident we'll have a tendency to immediately tell it with a certain degree of bias and emphasis. We might not even be aware we're doing it, but invariably we are. And to be fair it's unlikely we'll want to present ourselves in the worst possible light. As a consequence, when we're telling our version of events certain information may be completely left out and the context or background to the event entirely overlooked.

So it's helpful to understand that we can *all* be prone to putting our own particular angle on a story and have a tendency to subtly alter and distort the facts in our favour. Sometimes without realizing we're doing so.

That's why when it comes to succeeding with people we need to be especially aware of our own personal in-built bias to do this. So remind yourself that on occasions (I recognize not all) it does take two to tango.

In other words, despite me being able to convince myself that the entire blame for a conflict or disagreement lies with another person, I need to challenge myself to take a look at what role I may have also played in contributing to the situation. I'm not suggesting there's equal blame or responsibility to be apportioned. Just recognize that you may, perhaps unintentionally, have also added to the conflict.

How?

Well there could be a number of reasons.

You may have made some wrong assumptions. Your intentions may not have been clear to the other person. Perhaps you had previously said or done something which had upset them. This list could go on and on.

But here's the challenge.

Our own contribution to the conflict can be hard to see when we keep re-telling the story with our own particular spin on it. Through the continual repeating of a story we can begin to believe our version of events is a complete and accurate representation of all the facts.

Trust me, it never is.

Bite Size Wisdom

> Remember, life is rarely ever clear cut, black and white, right and wrong

In reality it's complex, confusing, messy and various shades of grey at times. And it's within that context we play out our relationships with others.

So be careful, because we can be prone at times to quickly play judge and jury in a situation and condemn people immediately as a result. However, that's like listening to the facts of a crime from the prosecution's perspective and reaching a verdict without listening to the case for the defence.

So tread with caution, because conflicts can escalate as a result of this blinkered approach. And an unwillingness to look at your own role in contributing to a particular misunderstanding or conflict can make a positive outcome harder to achieve.

Matthew, writing in the New Testament, quotes Jesus as saying the following:

> *"Why do you look at the speck of sawdust in your brother's eye and pay no attention to the plank in your own eye?" (Matthew 7: 3, New International Version.)*

Rather blunt I realize, but certainly worth reflecting on. Agree?

Bite Size Challenge

When was the last time you took a step back and asked "In what way is my behaviour contributing to this problem?"

No investment no return

I heard recently that a branch of a poorly performing retail store had been turned around by the introduction of a new manager.

That's not the most surprising thing you'll ever read is it?

But the next bit might be.

The hundred or so full- and part-time staff of the store reported one of the main reasons for their improved performance and increased morale was this:

The new manager used and remembered everyone's names.

They actually showed an interest in them as people, not just in their performance.

Now I'm sure there were many other things the new manager did to improve the performance of the store, but this seems to be the one that created the biggest impact on staff.

Not a pay rise. But remembering and using people's names.

Bite Size Wisdom

Never underestimate
the large impact of
a small gesture

In our never-stand-still, frenetic, multi-optional communication channel-filled world, it's easy to forget the following: The power and importance of investing time in a quiet, uninterrupted face-to-face conversation with someone.

You see the reality is that it's easy to see people every day and yet not really know them.

It's easy to allow significant relationships to simply drift along on auto-pilot rather than be lived out intentionally.

It's easy to allow what was a good, vibrant healthy relationship to fade and ultimately fizzle out.

Not deliberately.

Not maliciously.

But simply through neglect.

You stopped making the time to talk.

To listen.

To question.

To laugh.

To do things together.

As a team. As a couple. As a family.

And the reasons?

Perhaps you were busy. Perhaps they were. Maybe there were so many other distractions. Maybe because there seemed no real need to catch up properly. Everything seemed fine. There were no big issues to address.

"Hey, if it ain't broke, don't fix it" may be the attitude adopted by some. However, that's not quite the approach you would take with a car, is it? Even if it's running smoothly you still take it for a service. It makes good sense to do so. It's an opportunity to replace or repair parts *before* they cause any damage. Making such an investment not only prevents problems occurring in the future, it also lengthens the reliability and life of the car.

Common sense really.

Maybe we need to take such an approach with our relationships. Long-term customers may appreciate a visit, staff may value the opportunity to both give and receive feedback. Loved ones may enjoy doing some simple things together like going for a walk or having a relaxed uninterrupted conversation that gives them the opportunity to re-connect emotionally.

Here's the deal:

Bite Size Wisdom

Great relationships with customers, colleagues or loved ones don't just happen magically. They take time

Consciously or unconsciously, there are factors that contribute to the success of a relationship both in and outside of work. And when you fail to invest any time with people, don't be surprised when you fail to see any return. The harsh truth is being too comfortable and too complacent can kill a relationship. Being too busy and distracted can lead to a breakdown between people in both a professional and personal setting.

Never assume the honeymoon period will last.

It won't.

Trust me.

I've learnt that from experience.

The nature of my work means I can be away from home on a regular basis. I can easily go days and on occasions weeks without seeing my wife and children. When I come home after all my travelling I really appreciate a little bit of quiet downtime and readjustment.

The problem is that if I'm not careful this can become a habit. My downtime by myself can become normality. It can become the rule, not the exception.

So I have to make some choices. Conscious choices.

So, family meals are rarely if ever in front of the television, they're around our kitchen table. Time out with each other is diarized, not simply desired if we have time to squeeze it in.

With my son this has been easy to do. Our mutual love of football (if you can describe watching Wigan Athletic as football) determines that we'll often spend time together. Working with my wife also gives us the freedom and flexibility to take some time out with each other. And my mum has her weekly Wednesday night ritual when she comes round for dinner and lavishes the family with chocolate whilst reminding us to be careful with our weight. Mums, eh?

However, when my daughter Ruth was growing up it was different. We share few common interests. I gave up my love of makeup, handbags and high heels a long time ago. But I became aware by the time she reached her tenth birthday that the main focus of our conversation had by then invariably begun to revolve around the state of her bedroom (which to be fair did resemble the aftermath of a tsunami and earthquake combined). We were drifting apart. I needed to make some changes.

The length of time I spent away from home continued. But what I did when I was at home changed. Unlike previously, I no longer complained about being Ruth's taxi service. I saw that time in the car together as an opportunity for some natural, unforced conversation. We had the occasional meal out – just the two of us. She still spent some of that time on her phone but we did have some quality time together and she appreciated that. Until recently, once a year we would have a weekend together in London. I spoilt her and in return she helped me choose clothes that made me look at least one step removed from middle-aged meltdown.

Her bedroom remains untidy.

I fail to comprehend her taste in certain types of music. Going to concerts in order to be bashed around in a mosh pit is still alien to me.

And I'll probably pass on the tattoos and body piercing. For the time being, anyway.

But what we did laid down some solid foundations in terms of our relationship and we certainly created some good memories. We still do now, normally with short breaks abroad accompanied by her mum, or over dinner in rather more sophisticated eateries than when she was a teen.

Of course, I'm aware you might not have a son or daughter. However, whether you have or haven't is not the issue, because the principle remains the same with customers, colleagues and loved ones. No investment, no return.

If you really believe people are important (and my guess is you do, or else you wouldn't have read this far) then quit hoping to *find* the time to invest in those relationships. *Make* the time. And this next point is crucial. Remember, investing doesn't necessarily mean talking. Sometimes the most important thing can be simply doing things together and sharing the experience.

And if you're a manager, remember investing in people will also mean investing in their development. Recruiting talent can be a costly and time consuming exercise. But if you want to retain people, recognize that you will need to invest in them if you want to see a return on their talent.

Bite Size Wisdom

> Some managers say "What if we train people and they leave?" Well, what if you don't train people and they stay?

So invest some time with people, and look for ways to invest in their development as well. Oh, and if you're in a relationship with someone, ponder these powerful words by the author Phillip Yancey:

"The opposite of love is not hate. It's indifference."

Bite Size Challenge

Who in your world requires more of your time and attention right now? Choose someone not out of guilt but genuine desire to build a better relationship and diary some time together. Why not do that now rather than reading any further? Go on then.

Section Two

Move On

Have realistic expectations

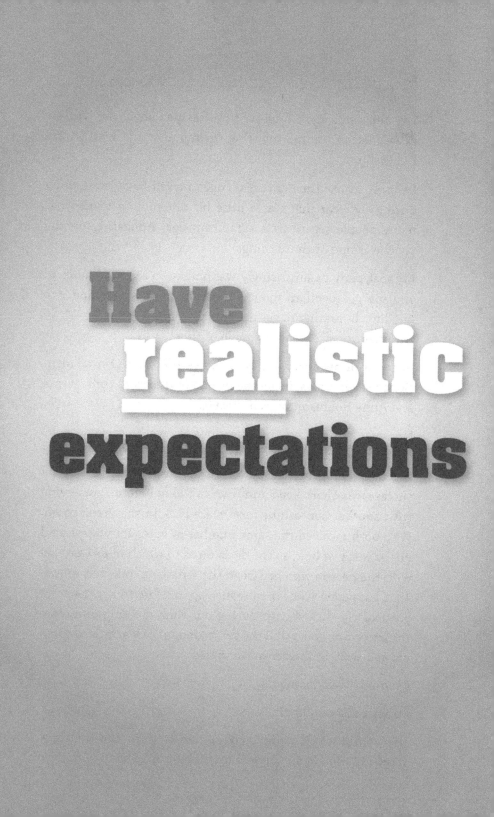

A few years ago I took part on the quiz show *The Weakest Link*, presented by the formidable TV host Anne Robinson.

I was 40 at the time and challenged myself to do something during the year that was a little bit different to mark what many people regard as a significant age. Appearing on the show was one of those things.

My goal, perhaps surprisingly, was not to win the show; quizzes and me go together about as well as mushy peas and rice pudding, but rather to get the phrase SUMO – "Shut Up, Move On" mentioned at least a couple of times.

In terms of my goal I was very successful. "SUMO" was mentioned seven times, including by one of the other contestants and Anne Robinson herself. Result.

However, answering the questions correctly proved to be more challenging. To my surprise I did make a good start and was the "strongest link" on one of the earlier rounds. But my success was short-lived and it wasn't long before I was vying with another contestant for a place back in the green room. We'd both received the same number of votes for who should be the weakest link, so the decision as to which of us went lay with the person who had been the strongest link that round. That happened to be a woman who, it's fair to say, I hadn't particularly clicked with during our time meeting up before the show. She generated the same amount of warmth towards me as a walk-in freezer in Antarctica.

I sensed I was doomed.

I wasn't disappointed.

The woman who'd pronounced sentence on me and thus triggered my walk of shame was then questioned as to why she'd voted me off. I wondered if it was related to my ridiculously stupid answer to a relatively simple question. Or was it due to the fact that she thought my ignorance was faked and was part of a cunning ploy and that I could actually be a potential threat in the later rounds?

No.

So what was her reason?

You'll never guess.

She'd once read a book on motivation and it didn't work for her, and knowing a little of my background she believed I deserved to go.

That was it.

End of story.

Anne Robinson took great pleasure in telling me it was time to shut up and move on as I was now the weakest link.

As I reflected on my arch enemy's reason for voting me off it caused me to wonder if in many ways her attitude sums up the attitudes of many people in regards to themselves, other people and perhaps life in general – ***"I tried it once and it didn't work."*** Yet no one really thinks they can get fit by going to the gym once. Or lose a certain amount of weight because they gave up burger and fries for a day. And yet in other areas of life we do seem to hold on to unrealistic and unreasonable expectations.

Perhaps at the root of some of our disappointments, frustrations and conflicts are the unrealistic expectations we have of other people and how they should respond and behave in situations.

At times we may even seek to justify these feelings by saying "I would never behave like that if I was them."

But that's the point.

You're not them.

You won't always know their history, their background, their values or who their own role models have been. You don't necessarily know what current challenges and concerns they may be facing, or insecurities they're struggling with.

In his book *Confessions of a Conjuror* (Transworld Publishers, 2010) Derren Brown puts it this way:

> *"Each of us is leading a difficult life, and when we meet people we are seeing only a tiny part of the thinnest veneer of their complex, troubled existence."*

OK, perhaps Derren is laying it on a little thick there, but I believe his words are worth reflecting on. Perhaps a little compassion and understanding on our part may be required at times.

Bite Size Wisdom

It's understandable that you want others to live up to your standards. But it's not always realistic

In relation to my "Weakest Link" opponent why would anyone think reading a book about motivation would magically transform them?

But they do.

Why would someone feel a complete lack of guilt about not giving their best at work?

But they do.

Why would someone make all kinds of promises to you without having the faintest intentions of actually delivering on them?

But they do.

Why do small children decide to have tantrums at the most inconvenient of times?

But they do.

So is this a call to lower your standards and raise a flag of surrender and passively accept whatever behaviour other people would care to throw in your direction?

No.

That's why this next point is crucial. Make sure you digest it.

Bite Size Wisdom

> "Realistic expectations" does not mean low expectations

I do believe that a lot of the time your expectations will be met; but let's not be so surprised when on occasions they're not. And if you can develop this "realistic mindset" when dealing with others you will become less frustrated and disappointed in people.

However, make sure that if your expectations are not met you ask yourself if that's due to them being unrealistically high or because you haven't actually clearly spelt out your expectations to others?

You see, I would love people to be as enthused as I am about personal development.

I would love everyone who hears me speak to be inspired, empowered and entertained.

But they're not.

In some cases (not too many, fortunately) it's the complete opposite.

Some people take an instant dislike to me and my material. If I could walk on water I'm convinced some people would turn round and say "that guy can't swim."

Reality rules.

And just as you can't please all of the people all of the time, similarly you won't be pleased by everyone all of the time.

It goes with the territory.

It's called life.

It's the reality of dealing with this amazing yet sometimes confusing and complex creature known as *Homo sapiens*. To an extent we're all weird, wacky and wonderful, although in what proportion varies from person to person. (You may know a few people who score particularly high on weird and wacky. My kids certainly think I do.)

However, the above doesn't mean we should automatically expect the worst from others. Let me stress it's good to have high expectations of yourself and other people and to strive for excellence. But don't make them unrealistically high.

Let's recognize and sometimes even embrace our flaws and the flaws of others. As a general principle, let's be more accepting rather than judgemental of others. However, don't compromise too much. Remember. . .

Bite Size Wisdom

Let's not be accepting of what is clearly unacceptable

Let's not abandon our standards, but be aware that it's not always realistic for everyone to meet them all of the time; especially from people who don't benefit from our age and experience.

Accept that there will be times when others will disappoint you. There will be times when others behave in a way very different to how you would. And when that happens, as I assure you it will, let's avoid making it into an unnecessary crisis or mini drama that causes us undue stress and anxiety and instead recognize sometimes you just need to SUMO: Shut Up, Move On.

Bite Size Challenge

Think of people who you feel have not met your expectations. Is that due to your expectations being unrealistic or because you didn't clearly communicate them?

zzzzzz

Let sleeping dogs lie ... sometimes

You may remember that in the earlier chapter "You get what you tolerate" we explored the challenges of tolerating and accepting other people's behaviour. This chapter is about the fact that on occasions it might be best to accept a situation or behaviour for the benefit of the long-term relationship.

Some may see this as contradictory advice.

It isn't.

As I mentioned previously, if you want to succeed with people you need to avoid a one-size-fits-all approach. Being flexible and adaptable is crucial to dealing with people, so sometimes a different approach or strategy is required. Remember, a fire extinguisher is very useful – but not if you're drowning. That's why on occasions a strategy to help you build a better long-term relationship could be to let sleeping dogs lie.

But what "things" might you want to tolerate?

That's for you to decide. But here are a few questions that might help you make your decision.

1. **What are the consequences of not tackling this issue? Am I happy and comfortable living with those consequences?**
2. **On a scale of 1–10 where 10 is extremely important, where would you rate your issue?**
3. **If you don't tackle the issue how important will it be in 6 months' time?**
4. **By leaving things as they are what message, if any, are you sending to others?**

5. **How strong a possibility is it that things will get worse if you say or do nothing?**
6. **Is it worth your time and energy addressing this issue in order to achieve what you want to achieve?**

It's also worth reflecting on this piece of wisdom:

Bite Size Wisdom

> Assertive people sometimes choose to be non-assertive

Perhaps the most important question to answer honestly in your own mind is: ***"By letting sleeping dogs lie am I comfortable both with the consequences of my decision and my reasons behind it?"***

Please don't use this idea as a way to justify a weakness on your part. This is not an excuse to avoid confrontation. It's not meant to be your starting point in all relationship issues, but a possible strategy you might use in order to ensure the long-term success of a relationship.

There are times when I reflect on my interactions with others and I think I made a mountain out of a molehill over some things. And there are some relationships which have never been the same because I decided to tackle an issue.

That's unfortunate, but it is reality.

Bite Size Challenge

> Has a previous decision you've made not to address an issue been a conscious choice on your part or because you lacked a little courage and didn't want to be seen as unpopular?

Perhaps it says more about the way I went about raising the problem than the actual problem itself (something we'll explore later in the book).

Equally, there are a number of relationships where I've kept my counsel, decided to bite my lip and which I'm so glad I did.

You see, not everything is worth fighting for.

Being totally transparent about your feelings in all situations is not always necessary. Choosing to lose the occasional battle in order to win the overall war can be an effective strategy. Choosing to be assertive all the time over every single issue is both tiring and boring. It can lead to issues escalating when they didn't need to, feelings being hurt and relationships being damaged.

Bite Size Wisdom

You don't always have to speak your mind. It's OK to shut up sometimes

Perhaps there may be an issue you're facing and it's best to let the scab heal on its own rather than continually picking at it.

Ultimately it's your call. Just remember, you do have choices.

Bite Size Challenge

Identify a current situation where you recognize it is probably better to let sleeping dogs lie.

Check out your attitude

I don't know if you've ever changed car, moved house or been pregnant (or known someone close to you who is). But if you have then you'll probably be aware of a strange phenomenon. Psychologists call it "attention awareness."

Let me explain.

When I was thinking of buying another car I suddenly started spotting that particular type of car everywhere. When I put my house up for sale, I then couldn't drive down a road without noticing "For Sale" signs. Neither could I read a newspaper or something online without stumbling across an article about houses. And when my wife was pregnant in the 1990s (not the whole decade I hasten to add – just two nine-month periods) she remarked on just how many women she'd noticed were also expecting at the same time.

Bite Size Wisdom

Your brain is incredibly skilled in helping you find what you're looking for

As humans we're very adept at noticing what is relevant or important to us at that particular time.

OK. Big deal, you might be thinking. So why is that fact important to you and me? Well, let's apply this same principle to how we are with people.

If you notice and talk about a particular positive or negative trait in another person you'll then continue to notice it (like I did with cars and houses, and my wife did with pregnant women). Once a habit or type of behaviour appears on your radar it's actually very difficult not to notice it in the future.

Consequently, if we're not careful we can actually develop a distorted picture of someone by either always noticing the positives, sometimes referred to as "the halo effect," or equally always noticing the negatives, which is referred to as "the horns effect." (The reason for horns is in connection with how the concept of the devil is often visually portrayed as having two horns.)

Now, if you're struggling in a relationship with someone there's an extremely high chance that you will tend to notice and talk about their negative behaviours.

That's understandable. But remember this:

What you focus on magnifies.

And so begins a cycle. Your negative attitude towards someone is fuelled by you noticing negative things about them which in turn reinforces your negative views of them:

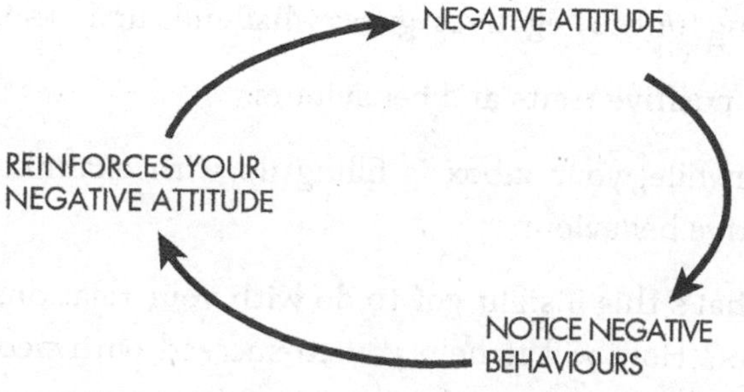

Bite Size Wisdom

> In many ways your view of people becomes a self-fulfilling prophecy

Not only that, but if you're not looking for the positives in people you won't notice them.

So why's that the case?

It's all to do with how your brain works.

Aware of just how much information your mind is being bombarded with, the brain's attempt to help us avoid a mental meltdown is in many ways similar to an email spam filter. It filters out information that is not considered life threatening, relevant or highly unusual. And that all goes in the junk box.

And your attitude determines what goes in the junk box unopened.

So if you're ***not*** looking for the positives in people and only looking for the negatives, guess what ends up in the junk box?

Their positive traits and behaviours.

Meanwhile, your inbox is filling up with examples of their negative behaviour.

So what's this insight got to do with your relationships with others? How will it help you to succeed with people? Well, think of a person you don't get on with as well as you would like. Here are some questions to reflect on.

- **What is it about their behaviour you don't particularly like?**
- **Is it possible you only notice their negative behaviour and fail to notice any of their more positive traits?**
- **What are the consequences of having a negative attitude towards them?**
- **If you had to acknowledge three positive traits about the person what would they be?**

I'm not suggesting reflecting on these questions has now filled you with warm fuzzy feelings towards this other person. However, it might have led you to opening your junk mail and realizing there are some positive things about them that you may not have noticed before.

OK, now let me share with you an important and painful lesson from my own experience, which illustrates the dangers of having a fixed negative view of someone and how your attitude affects your behaviour. As you're about to see, my experience would have been very different if I'd only thought about the previous questions.

Several years ago I was working with a company who were set up to support organizations who were making people redundant. I was hired to offer advice and support to staff who were losing their jobs.

Over time I got to know some people particularly well as I helped them compile CVs and coached them on interview techniques. Some of those people are now a distant memory, but there was one guy I'll never forget.

Mark.

He was a challenge.

The best way to describe him was that he was like a leech. He seemed to latch on to me and drain me of my life, my energy and my reasons for living. Five minutes with Mark felt like five hours with someone else.

It's fair to say he didn't exactly light up my life when he walked into my office.

Quite the opposite in fact.

It became quite a joke amongst other members of the team. Comments such as "I see your friend's in to see you later" were commonplace. And despite all my efforts to help Mark he remained unsuccessful in finding work. So he visited our offices even more.

Then I got some great news.

Mark had set himself up in business. Finally, he would be off my books. Finally, I would look at my appointment book without the sense of dread I had felt previously. Life felt good all of a sudden.

In a fit of overwhelming generosity I bought the three admin staff a small chocolate bar.

Each.

I returned to my own office with a sense of renewed optimism about life. In fact, if you'd asked me at that point could the England football team win a match on penalties at a major football tournament I would have probably answered "yes."

That's how good and optimistic I felt.

And then within moments my joyous world evaporated before me. As I looked out across the car park from my office window I saw a large white van pull up.

And Mark got out.

He walked towards our office.

I dashed back into reception to confront Vera the receptionist.

She had finished her chocolate bar.

"Vera, Vera," I squeaked, in a slightly startled "this isn't really happening to me" kind of voice.

"I've just seen Mark. He's heading here right now."

"Didn't you know?" Vera enquired in a rather casual, non-plussed way.

"Didn't I know what?" I replied, already beginning to regret my decision to buy those bars of chocolate.

"Well as part of our ongoing service to Mark, he's going to be using our office as his office. He'll be using our stamps, our stationery, our photocopier. In fact, we should be seeing a lot more of him."

I was dumbstruck.

For once.

My brain struggled to process what Vera was telling me. And then in the darkness of my confusion there came a brief shaft of light.

Hide.

If I hid in the gents' toilets, Vera could tell Mark I'd gone out for lunch and he'd have to see one of my colleagues instead.

Not, I confess, an idea I'm particularly proud of in hindsight, but it seemed like a good one at the time.

However, I had no time to implement it. Before I knew it Mark was stood next to me.

"Alright Paul. How you doing?"

Despite my face portraying a deep sense of doom and gloom I managed to squeeze out a muted reply.

"Yeah, fine thanks."

"Good. I was wondering if I could see you then?"

"Have you made an appointment?" A question I asked despite already knowing the answer, as I'd already seen the appointment book.

"No, I just thought I'd pop in and see you."

I struggled to hide my displeasure at seeing him (and the fact that I'd bought those three bars of chocolate needlessly).

"Well to be honest, Mark, you should have made an appointment. I could have been seeing another client. As it is, I'm just about to go for lunch."

"So can I see you then?" he persevered.

"Go on then" I replied reluctantly.

I took him into my office.

I sat down.

He sat down.

Then he said something I'll never forget.

"I won't keep you long as I know you don't like me."

I was stunned.

I tried to regain my composure. I muttered some response along the lines of "don't be so ridiculous." But Mark had rumbled me. He'd sussed me out.

Bite Size Wisdom

Your attitude affects your behaviour and the way in which you communicate

From that day on things changed between me and Mark. I realized I had allowed my attitude towards him to move into the realms of complacency and indifference.

I had stopped being professional.

I had forgotten that I was being paid to serve Mark. Without any clients my services would not be required. It was because of people like Mark that I had work.

I had forgotten that.

I'd slipped into an attitude whereby I provided great service to the people I liked.

And because of my negative attitude towards Mark I found it rather easy to notice the things I didn't like about him.

So if I wanted to change my relationship with him I needed to change my attitude towards him. I started to look more for the positives. His work ethic. His willingness to take risks and start his own business.

And you know what?

It worked.

There was no moving reconciliation.

There were no tears.

But things got better between us. He became friendlier and less intense. We talked more about solutions to his business challenges rather than dwelling simply on the problems he faced.

Was it perfect? No. But it was better. He never challenged me about not liking him again, and I actually found seeing him a more enjoyable experience.

He hadn't changed particularly.

But my attitude towards him had. And as a result we developed a more successful professional relationship.

Bite Size Challenge

- So is your attitude towards someone hindering your relationship with them?
- Are you so blinded by the negatives you see in them that you're failing to see any positives?
- What's a small change in behaviour you can make to create a more positive (not perfect) relationship between you? Think of a specific thing you will do next time you interact with that person.

Be willing to be wrong

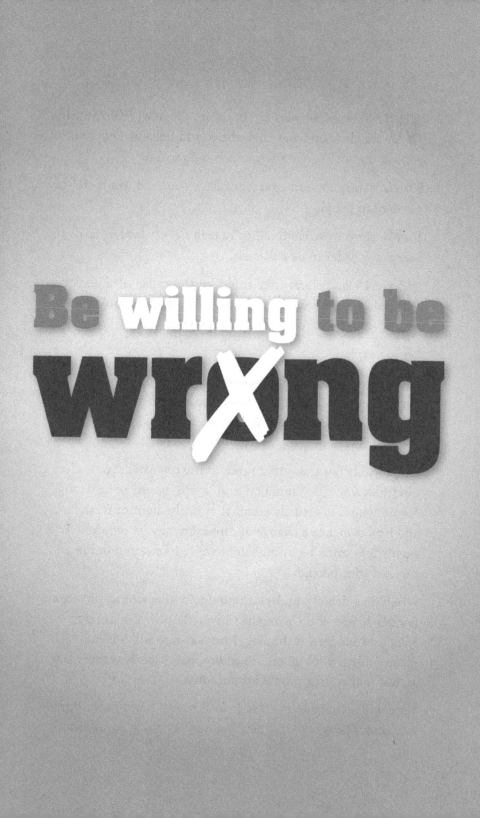

We like people who are decisive, don't we? People who are clear on what they think and believe. People who don't dither or change their minds on a whim.

Focus, determination and confidence are all traits to be admired in people

They're signs of strength. They're traits every leader needs to possess in order to be a success.

And yet I also believe they could be the cause of a person's downfall. As contradictory as this sounds, they could be the reason why we don't succeed with people.

Let me explain.

Focus could lead to being blinkered in your approach. Determination could result in a stubbornness to change despite what the facts are telling us. Confidence could lead to a dangerous cocktail of arrogance and complacency.

It's probably fair to say that rarely at the top of a list of leaders' top traits would be "humility" and "a willingness to be wrong." A willingness to actually admit that in the light of fresh facts and new evidence a change of direction may be required. But such traits could be invaluable if we're to succeed in life and succeed with people.

When I'm driving and start going in the wrong direction (which happens on a regular basis despite the support of advanced modern technology) my sat-nav will advise me to make a U-turn. To ignore its advice, particularly when I'm in an unfamiliar area, would be stupidity.

Yet some political leaders, such as Britain's first female Prime Minister Margaret Thatcher, baulked at such an approach.

To make a U-turn was seen by her as a sign of political weakness. In some cases it probably was.

In some cases.

But ultimately an unwillingness on her part to ever admit she was wrong meant she lost the loyalty and respect of some of those closest to her, and this led to her unceremonious and premature departure as leader of her own party.

A similar stubbornness was fortunately demonstrated by Adolf Hitler. I say fortunately, because if he had been prepared to listen more to his generals and adopt a more flexible approach to Germany's war efforts then he may have tragically achieved the political outcome he was striving for.

Bite Size Wisdom

There may only be a subtle difference between "determination" and "stubbornness," but one leads to success whilst the other makes you look stupid

I'm not suggesting we abandon focus, determination and confidence. But I am suggesting this:

An overused strength can actually become a weakness.

However, this is not a call to embrace the complete opposite of these traits. But it is a challenge to be willing to temper them with a mixture of humility and openness when required.

Bite Size Challenge

How open and willing are you to having your ideas challenged by others? When was the last time you actively sought out someone to do so?

The reality is we need to be careful of becoming too black and white in our thinking about *every* issue.

Sometimes grey is OK.

Uncertainty goes with the territory in our ever changing world, and in order to embrace that uncertainty successfully, we have to be more open and flexible in our thinking and approach. That in a nutshell is often the key to succeeding with people.

OK, so what does this mean in practice?

It could mean not always trusting your gut feeling. Trust me; your gut feeling is not always right on every issue – particularly when you don't have all the facts to hand.

When you're meeting other people please remember first impressions are not always right either. They're powerful, and they're influential, but they're not always correct. But here's our challenge. We all have a propensity to jump to conclusions about people in our quest to pigeonhole them. We like putting people in boxes. It gives us a greater feeling of control. But this need to do so can have its downsides.

As you're about to discover.

Trusting my gut and going with "my first impression" has literally cost me thousands of pounds.

I've ended up working with people I should never have worked with. I've made important and significant decisions in my business and lived to regret them because I placed too much emphasis on my feelings and not enough on facts.

Once I'd made a decision I wasn't especially open to the possibility that I may be wrong. I persisted working with people I should have moved on from.

Big mistake.

To quote a proverb of the Dakota people:

"When you're riding a dead horse, dismount."

I'm not suggesting you ignore your feelings, but please be aware how much they can fluctuate.

So why not try this approach in future: Pre-empt your comments by saying "I may be wrong on this, but this is how I currently feel about things."

This encourages others to contribute their opinion without feeling they're attacking your position. It also gives you a get-out-of-jail card which gives you the opportunity to change your opinion on a matter.

Clearly to do so all the time means you start to lose credibility, and in a time of real crisis this approach would do little to inspire confidence in others. But a willingness to be wrong and an openness to listen to and explore others' views and thoughts can be invaluable . . . sometimes. It's a great way to increase the engagement of others when you take such an approach and encourages others to share their own insights and ideas.

Fortunately, a willingness to be wrong did contribute to the success of one of my bestselling books, *Self-Confidence*. That was the title my publisher came up with. I much preferred what I considered to be the far more quirky, engaging and sexy title *You Don't Have to Dance Naked*, with the subtitle *The real truth on how to develop your confidence*. Most of my friends agreed. In contrast the publisher's title was both boring and bland.

However, I had to confess my publisher had a better understanding of the market than I did. They knew that the main book buyer of a well-known retailer in the UK would not support a book called *You Don't Have to Dance Naked*. It was just too quirky a title for them and the market they were aiming at.

But I had a gut feeling.

People would love the title. The word "naked" in the title would immediately arouse curiosity and interest.

But in the end I put my gut feelings to one side. I listened to my publisher. I went with their advice. I was willing to be wrong.

The question is, are you too?

So was my publisher right? Was my willingness to be wrong justified?

Well my book *Self-Confidence* was published in January 2010. It spent 24 weeks at number one in a particular UK retailer's business chart. It was quickly snapped up by a number of foreign publishers and is now available in several languages.

Who knows how well my alternative title would have done.

Even better perhaps? I doubt it.

My gut feeling was wrong.

It won't be all the time. And it would be stupid to ignore it. But it would also be stupid to make it the sole arbitrator of all my decisions.

Bite Size Wisdom

> It's not a sign of weakness to admit you may be wrong; it's often a sign of wisdom

You need to weigh up your facts and not just your feelings. You need to listen to people who see the world differently to you. You won't always agree, but it would be unwise not to listen.

And when people feel they work for or live with someone who is prepared to listen to their perspective even when it may be different from their own, that can be highly motivating.

Agree?

Bite Size Challenge

Do you encourage people to challenge your thinking and viewpoint? Are you willing to admit you're wrong sometimes?

Don't

treat people as you want to be

treated

It seems on the surface such a noble suggestion: treat people as you would want to be treated. And to be fair it's pretty good advice.

Up to a point.

Treating people with the degree of respect and courtesy that we would appreciate does seem a fairly reasonable starting place when dealing with others.

But please don't fall into the trap of thinking that what floats your boat also floats mine.

In fact, treating people as you want to be treated could have disastrous consequences and be the reason why you don't succeed with people.

Let me elaborate.

Kev is a key member of my team. He's quiet, intelligent, and also a little shy. Now, if you want to show your appreciation for something I have done then it's not stretching the point too much to say I can cope with some public recognition. And without trying to appear arrogant and conceited (which I realize I probably will) I quite enjoy being the centre of attention.

In fact, "enjoy" is not totally accurate.

I relish it.

Hey, that's how I am wired. I'm not expecting undying adoration and people throwing bouquets of flowers at me. Neither am I suggesting I want to be the sole focus of attention. But I'm comfortable with all eyes being focused on me. I'm a professional speaker after all. I thrive in such situations. I love making people laugh and meeting new people. It gives me a buzz.

Now let's go back to Kev. He sometimes accompanies me on my speaking engagements. If I wanted to show how much I valued him the last thing he would want is public recognition.

Call him up on stage and I doubt his legs would get him there. He would prefer the ground to swallow him up. He'd be embarrassed. It might well rank as one of his top ten awful moments on planet Earth. His cry would be echoed in this next piece of wisdom:

Bite Size Wisdom

> Whatever you do, don't treat everyone the way you want to be treated

That's good to ponder isn't it? How often do we assume that what we'd appreciate others will too?

Well, we'd be right.

Some of the time.

But there may be occasions when the opposite is the case.

I value Kev as part of my team, but I won't be organizing a big party in his honour and then inviting him up on stage to say a few words. I want him to remain a key player in the team, not resentful towards me for putting him through such an ordeal. (And Kev, if you are reading this, I promise I never will, OK?)

This insight has also proved invaluable in my relationship with my wife Helen. If I've received some bad news I like space. I need to be alone. I may go for a walk which gives me the opportunity to process my thoughts and come to terms with what I've heard.

After that I'm ready to talk to others.

Helen is different. When she's heard some bad news she wants to talk. If I gave her space and time to be on her own she might interpret that as not caring.

If I treat Helen as I would like to be treated I actually could cause a degree of pain and hurt. So although I walk, she prefers to talk. That's fine. We each respect that we both handle certain situations differently from each other, and over time we've learnt to respect that fact.

And this insight applies equally if you have children. It's certainly helped me in my relationship with my daughter Ruth, who I talked about earlier. Helen, my son Matt and I are fairly tactile. We're comfortable hugging both privately and in public. Helen and I have been known to kiss occasionally, and even hold hands (although usually only when there's a full moon).

Ruth my daughter is different.

Very different.

From an early age she made it very clear that "I don't like hugs and kisses."

Personally I didn't find that easy. I like to show my affection towards her. The only problem is, she doesn't like receiving it in the way I like to show it! But if I want to build a good relationship with my daughter then I need to treat her as she wants to be treated. Which means hugs and kisses are rarely on the menu.

However, Ruth has made it clear that expressions of affection in the form of buying her clothes, handbags and shoes are perfectly acceptable to her!

Now although the above may appear amusing, it has taken me time to adjust my expectations. However, I've learnt the following valuable lesson as a result of my relationship with Ruth:

Bite Size Wisdom

> If you want to succeed with others focus on meeting their needs first rather than your own

Perhaps your relationship with someone has stalled because you've not taken time to consider what it is they see as important and what they would value. This applies equally at work as it does at home. Don't assume people value the same things as you. Our personalities are different, our interests could be, and perhaps more importantly so could what does and doesn't motivate us. Remember, what fits you might not fit them, so start treating people as *they* want to be treated.

And if you're not sure how people want to be treated, ask. Far better to ask than simply assume. So make sure you check out the following questions, as the answers could prove key to understanding how to develop more positive relationships both in and outside the workplace.

Bite Size Challenge

A great way to understand what motivates people and "floats their boat" is to ask these questions:

- In order for you to feel valued and appreciated by someone, what would they need to do to demonstrate that?
- What brings you most satisfaction from work?
- Describe a time when you felt particularly motivated at work. Why did you feel motivated?
- Is there one thing I could do to support you that I'm not currently doing?

Now over to you. Which of the questions do you need to ask to some of the key people in your life? When do you intend doing so?

How to make change a success

If you're going to succeed with people then you'll need to know how to help them deal with change. And if you can master the skills to do so, that will prove invaluable to you in both your personal and professional life.

We explored earlier why change is complicated. There are times when it's positively embraced, but equally there are occasions when it's fiercely resisted.

Whatever the reasons for people's resistance, this chapter focuses on five approaches you can take to make change less scary and more successful.

Five ways to make change a success

1. Give clarity.

When people feel in the dark, they're invariably drawn to the most negative conclusions about a situation.

Bite Size Wisdom

> Silence creates an environment where people speculate, and anxiety escalates

So, giving people clarity is crucial. Without it you create conditions where rumours flourish, and they're rarely of the positive variety.

To counter this, you need to be as clear as you can be with people about the situation you're facing. Otherwise it's like asking people to do a jigsaw without them knowing what the end picture looks like.

Remember, the fundamental question people need answering is this. . .

"How will this change affect me?"

The sooner you can answer that question for someone the better. Even if the news is bad, at least people know where they stand.

If you want change to be less scary for people, do all you can to prevent them having to swim in a sea of uncertainty. Or as my straight-talking friend Denise says, "People are not mushrooms – don't keep them in the dark and cover them in shit!" (She never did graduate from Charm School, but actually her bluntness is what some people need to hear.)

As we explored earlier, in order to provide clarity, explain the reasons for the change, the consequences of not doing it, and, when you can, the benefits that come as a result of it. If you can't find a direct benefit for them, then don't patronize people by pretending there are any. Life isn't always as simple as that, and most people have a finely attuned bullshit detector.

Oh, and here's another question people have. . .

"What's expected of me?"

Bite Size Wisdom

> Clarity creates confidence, even in challenging times

During the Covid 19 pandemic people craved clarity. They wanted answers to such questions as "What do we need to do, or stop doing, and for how long?"

Admittedly the goalposts kept moving, but at least there were goalposts to move in the first place.

Here's the deal: a lack of clarity breeds confusion. I recognize you may be constrained in being totally transparent in your communication with people at times, especially in a work context, but always aim to shed as much light on a situation as possible. (Remember, they're not mushrooms.) If you cannot offer clarity now, let people know when you will be able to do so.

And be honest. Sometimes you can't offer clarity because you yourself are unclear. If that's the case, admit it, and don't be surprised at people's reactions. They're not being negative, they're being normal.

2. Develop people's competence.

When I transitioned from speaking in person to presenting online, there was a huge deficit in terms of my ability to use the necessary technology. In fact, not only was I lacking the skills to use it, I didn't even own much of what was required. My laptop was ancient (acquired at a car boot sale from a bloke called Noah) and I had never used a webcam prior to March 2020. I'm the guy who was so unfamiliar with technology I rarely made Skype calls and had never even heard of Zoom. I felt about as comfortable with technology as a vegan at a barbecue.

I don't think my experience was uncommon. The specifics may be different, but people will feel threatened and insecure when they're out of their comfort zone and are lacking the tools, technology, and training to meet new challenges. That's why people need reassurance that support will be available.

Equally, it's also important to recognize that people will vary from each other in how quickly they come up to speed with new changes. Whilst some people adjust like a chocaholic in a sweet shop, others are more like a giraffe on roller skates. And I definitely felt like that giraffe when I had to transform the way I operated my business.

How did I navigate such a period? Simple. I turned to my colleagues and my wife (who works in my business) for support. Every day felt like a school day, which for someone in their late fifties took some adjusting to. But I got there.

3. Nurture confidence.

I'm not saying confidence is crucial to people's success, but I did write a whole book on the subject.

Now here's the interesting thing about confidence – it's primarily rooted in competence and experience. It's not some magical mysterious gift that the gods bestow upon you at birth. It's far more mundane than that.

The reality is, if I'm good at something and I've done it a lot of times then confidence naturally develops. That's why when change happens and you're asked to do something new or different – which may mean you need to learn new skills or processes – your confidence is understandably not as high as it was previously.

That's why when people are going through change and doing something new, they need plenty of feedback and encouragement.

And if you find people are struggling initially, this next point is really important to remember.

Bite Size Wisdom

> Help people to focus on progress, not perfection

Change can be messy. So when there are signs of success, broadcast them. It's unlikely that if someone is doing a new task or is in a new role that they'll achieve mastery from day one. It can be a humbling experience, especially for more experienced people, to adopt a new way of working, particularly if they're having to learn or get support from someone younger or more junior to them. But whatever people's position or experience. . .

Bite Size Wisdom

We all need the oxygen of encouragement

Nurture people's confidence and you'll help reduce their anxiety and increase their courage to embrace change.

4. Give control. . .when possible.

As we saw earlier, we all crave a degree of autonomy. We don't like to be controlled by others – although if you're living in North Korea you haven't got much say in the matter.

So, if people are to positively embrace change it helps if they've been consulted and involved in as many aspects of the change as possible.

For instance, as many organizations move to a more hybrid way of working, allowing people some autonomy on which days they work from home gives them a greater sense of control over their working lives.

Bite Size Wisdom

> When you give people a choice, they feel more in control

This can be the case even when there are constraints to the choice. For example, "You can work from home two days a week, but you're required to be in the office every Wednesday."

Now, not every change can be implemented via a democratic decision or giving people choices. We weren't consulted when the country was tackling the Covid 19 pandemic, and the final say on some strategic decisions your organization needs to make might not be down to its employees – but still, do all you can to involve people in the process.

Remember, when there is an opportunity to give people some control, no matter how small it might be, take it.

And guess what?

This idea can even be applied to young children.

"Do you want a drink before or after you've cleared up your toys?"

Genius, eh?

(That tip alone is surely worth the price of the book!)

5. Help people feel cared for.

A fundamental human need we all have is the need to know we matter. Unfortunately, I've come across organizations who are going through change but focus solely on upgrading their technology and systems, and totally forget their people.

Then they wonder why the change wasn't a success or took so long to implement.

So, it's vitally important that if you're going to help people deal positively with change, they need to feel cared for. In other words, treat them as people, not just numbers (or mushrooms).

Now, if this all sounds a little pink and fluffy to you, let's see what that looks like in reality.

Here goes.

Make sure you create space for people to voice any concerns they have. This could be done anonymously, through a third party, in writing, or face to face. Keep people informed as much as possible. It's better to over-communicate than not to communicate enough. Remind people of the reasons why change is happening, and the role they play in making it happen. Be prepared to be both visible and available, even if that's done virtually. Never undervalue the power of a one-to-one conversation or a team briefing. In fact, you may want to circulate this next statement to everyone you know who has any responsibility for leading and influencing people.

In a world of iPhones and iPads, never underestimate the importance and impact of eyeballs.

And as my friend and fellow speaker Geoff Ramm says. . .

Bite Size Wisdom

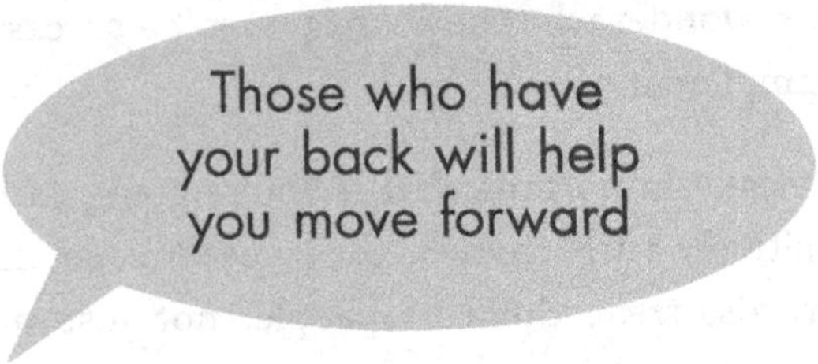
Those who have
your back will help
you move forward

That's what you want people to think about you.

The question is, do the people in your world know that you have their back?

So that's five ways to make change a success and a more positive and less scary experience for people.

Let's do a quick recap of them:

1. **Give clarity.**
2. **Develop competence.**
3. **Nurture confidence.**
4. **Give control. . . when possible.**
5. **Help people feel cared for.**

Bite Size Challenge

Identify one of the five ways to make change a success and reflect on how you can apply it to support someone (or a group of people) in your world. And if you're struggling with change, which of these five factors would be of most help to you right now?

Four killer questions you have to ask yourself

Right, in this chapter it's over to you. The ball is being placed very firmly in your court. I'll serve the questions, but it's how you respond to them that will determine whether you move on to develop better and more effective strategies in how you deal with people.

While most books promise to give you the answers, I promise in this chapter I won't. But the answers *you* come up with could prove to be some of the most enlightening and insightful you'll gain from reading this book.

Here's the deal. In a moment I'm going to pose you four questions. Don't rush through them. And don't be intimidated either. This is not a test. There are no right and wrong answers. You don't even have to write your answers down or share them with anyone, although you might find it beneficial to do so.

This is simply between me and you.

To begin with I want you to think of a person with whom your relationship is of some importance. This could be someone connected to your work, for example, a colleague, your boss, a supplier, a customer. It's the kind of relationship where a breakdown or a problem between you would have consequences. So I'm not suggesting you bring to mind the woman you're on nodding terms with on the tube or train, or the guy you buy your sandwiches from at lunchtime.

Alternatively, the person you might want to think of as you go through the questions may have nothing to do with work. Perhaps it's a close friend, your partner (or ex-partner), a relative or even one of your children. It's probably not Aunt Kathy who you last saw 27 years ago, only keep in contact with at Christmas and have to think twice before you remember if she's even alive.

Get the picture?

Good.

Now with this person in mind reflect on these four questions:

1. What's going on in their world at the moment?

It's so easy to be wrapped up in our world and in our priorities that we fail to show sufficient interest in others. It's hard to connect with others and to build rapport when you have no idea about their world.

I'm not suggesting you do too much delving or ask them to lie down on a couch and ask them about their childhood. But I am asking you to take some time to reflect on this question. Perhaps it challenges you to stop and pause for a moment. Guess what? Not everyone is as fascinated about your work and your family as you are. Some people quite like to talk about themselves occasionally. Your answer to this question may possibly reveal some reasons as to why this person is behaving the way they are at the moment.

Now I appreciate some people are very private. They like to keep themselves to themselves. They wouldn't want to discuss what's going on in their lives. Fine. But that's not everyone. And if at this stage you realize your answer to this question is a little sketchy then perhaps that's an indication you should spend a little more time asking about them rather than simply talking about yourself.

2. What's important to them at this time?

Here are some possible things that might be important to people at the moment.

Maybe this person would really value some feedback on how they're doing at work at present. Maybe they just need some uninterrupted time with you. Perhaps they need a good listening to. Maybe they need some support or advice regarding a particular challenge they're facing at the moment.

Or it could be the complete opposite. Perhaps they just need some space and to be left alone at the moment. They could actually value you toning down your interest in them at times. (This is what I discovered with my teenage daughter, who doesn't want to talk much when she's with her friends and who frankly doesn't have a compelling need to answer my question "So what've you done today?")

Some people may not be performing to their usual high standards because they no longer feel valued or appreciated. Is it possible someone you know might be feeling a little taken for granted at the moment? Could even as little as 30 minutes' one-to-one conversation over a coffee make them feel far more valued? And could this change in how they feel lead to a change in how they act and behave?

Of course you could do some educated guessing around this question, or perhaps your relationship is such that you could ask the person directly.

For example, you could ask "If there is one thing that you'd value me knowing that would make our relationship even better or easier what would it be?"

It's your call, just make sure you do consider this question.

3. Am I listening to understand or listening to defend?

The author Dan Rockwell says, **"The road to excellence is paved with tough conversations."** I think he's got a point.

The reality is that there are going to be times when in order to improve your relationship with others it will involve some potentially tricky and possibly difficult conversations. Let's not pretend these will be easy. They never are.

If someone is being quick to criticize you it's understandable that you'll be quick to defend. So the best way to perhaps de-escalate an issue is for you to simply shut up. Literally.

The other person could, as far as you're concerned, be speaking complete nonsense, but they still need to be heard. On the other hand, they may have a valid argument and provide an insight that you were unaware of.

Bite Size Wisdom

If you want problems to escalate make sure you hammer home why you're right and they're wrong. It works every time

The reality is that listening to understand rather than defend in these conversations won't be easy, but try lowering your defences, even just a little bit.

Perhaps you both have valid points. Perhaps there's just been a misunderstanding between you. So try listening to what the other person has to say rather than lowering the shutters in your mind. Ask questions when you need clarification. And when you can agree with a point, say so.

Bite Size Wisdom

> It's difficult to sustain anger with someone who's agreeing with you and trying to understand you

Here's an important point to remember though.

Listening to understand doesn't mean you'll always automatically agree with the other person's viewpoint. It simply means you're trying to understand their perspective. And when this happens they are then far more likely to listen to your point of view.

In my own relationship with my wife this particular question has proved both challenging and helpful. When Helen feels the need to give me . . .

how can I put this diplomatically . . .

"feedback"

my natural response is to listen whilst building up the case for the defence.

However, when I try to simply understand where she's coming from there have been numerous occasions when I've realized she has a valid point and I've needed to apologize. I'd like to say this is how we always resolve our differences, but the reality is that a combination of pride, emotions and fatigue mean we don't always adopt such an approach.

But when we do any potential conflict is invariably nipped in the bud.

Bite Size Challenge

How often do you consciously seek to understand someone else's viewpoint rather than automatically defend your own?

4. Have I clearly communicated my perspective?

The first three questions have been deliberately intended to help you focus on the other person's perspective and what's important to them. However, could the relationship between you both be helped by you clearly communicating your perspective?

Are you assuming that people know your priorities? Your agenda? Your needs?

Are you so clear in your own mind why a certain course of action needs to be taken that you've forgotten or overlooked the fact that others might not share your same clarity of vision?

Perhaps rather than simply telling people what needs to be done we need to spend a little more time explaining the "why." You might clearly see the reason why a certain action needs to be taken but others might not.

Bite Size Wisdom

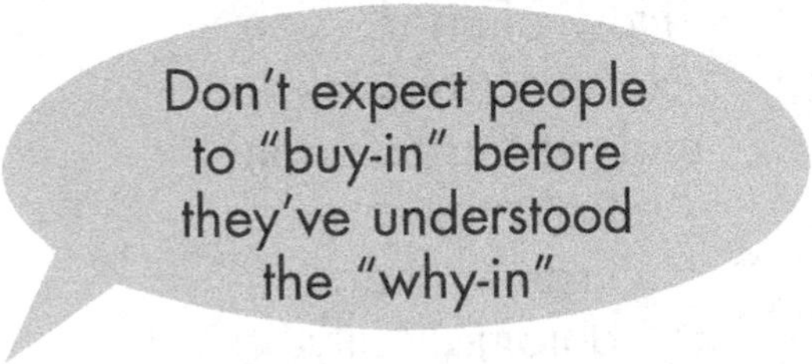
Don't expect people to "buy-in" before they've understood the "why-in"

Remember they might not currently have all the insights or facts on a situation you have. They might not appreciate the consequences of taking or not taking certain actions. And being told once about something is no guarantee they'll remember. Communicating your perspective may actually mean in practice reinforcing and reminding people of it. Regularly.

Here's a recap of the four questions:

1. **What's going on in their world at the moment?**
2. **What's important to them at this time?**
3. **Am I listening to understand or listening to defend?**
4. **Have I clearly communicated my perspective?**

Now having reflected on these questions, which were particularly useful to consider? All of them? Or one in particular?

OK, so what do you do with your answers and insights? Well that's up to you. I'm here to ask the questions. What you do or don't do with your answers is entirely your choice. But if I'm honest the exercise has been pointless if you fail to do anything as a result.

Agree?

Over to you then.

Bite Size Challenge

As a result of working through those four questions, what one specific action do you now need to take, and with whom?

How to make criticism count... not crucify

Have you ever received criticism or had to give feedback to anyone? It's not easy, is it? In fact, people go on courses to learn how to give and receive feedback. I've delivered some myself.

One in particular springs to mind.

I was working just outside London, running a workshop on "Getting the best from people" and we were exploring the subject of giving feedback. This can be reasonably straightforward when what you have to say is generally positive, but can be as difficult as running through quicksand when it's not. Sensitivity, diplomacy, being balanced and constructive can all be required when the feedback you're giving could also be construed as criticism.

Let's not fool ourselves either into thinking that putting the word "constructive" before the word "criticism" makes it any easier for people to receive. It doesn't. No matter how self-assured an individual may be, they, like the rest of us, have a tendency to fast forward past the word "constructive" and to pause on the word "criticism."

Do we really care that the criticism will be constructive? Rarely. Ultimately, no matter how much you're going to try and package what you're about to say, it's still criticism. And when you use the word "criticism" it invariably triggers the raising of defences in most people (with the possible exception of politicians, who seem immune to it due to the excessive amount they receive).

That's why at my workshop I had been at pains to point out the pitfalls of using certain words when giving feedback. I recommend people to stay well clear of words such as "weaknesses" and bin altogether the phrase "constructive criticism."

So I have to say I was rather surprised by how Ian, one of the participants on my course, responded to a question.

I had asked the group to consider how they would approach someone whose performance they wanted to improve. I was encouraged by the responses of many of the group. Then it came to Ian's turn.

"Well I would tell my team member, Ben, that he has the potential not to be crap."

For a moment I thought Ian was joking. But I quickly realized he wasn't.

"Do you want to think of your use of language there Ian, and the impact of the words you use?" I asked.

"What, the word 'potential'?" replied Ian, with just a hint of sarcasm in his voice.

Now, Ian might be an extreme example (and I really do hope he was joking), but how many of us have had our confidence knocked by what someone has said or written about us?

Bite Size Wisdom

> Never underestimate the long-term effect of just a few brief words

Challenging people without undermining their confidence is not easy, particularly when you're having to do so with someone who is young and inexperienced. But there are of course those that go to the other end of the spectrum and sugar-coat their criticism to such an extent that the person hearing it thinks they've just been paid a compliment. Rather than challenge people about a piece of work or the way they're behaving we've ended up so wanting to avoid upsetting them that they feel they've just received a big cuddle, not a mild rebuke.

So is there a middle way? Is there a way of giving "constructive criticism" without actually having to use the phrase?

You'll be relieved to know there is.

Firstly, let's be clear in our own mind that our focus has to be on solving issues, not fixing blame.

Bite Size Wisdom

We want our words
to build up people,
not beat up people

Here's a great strategy to do just that. I first came across this approach during my time working for the Chief Executive group Vistage (if you want to find out more about them please go to `www.vistage.co.uk`).

Like the best and most effective things in life, it's rather straightforward. Here goes.

When giving someone feedback, point out the positives by talking about ***"what worked well"*** and giving some specific examples. Point to any potential negatives or areas for improvement by beginning with the phrase ***"even better if . . ."*** and highlight how things can improve.

For example: "What worked well was the start of your presentation when you immediately engaged your audience by asking us a question." "Even better if you gave more thought to how you ended your presentation, perhaps by summarizing your main points and challenging us with one specific action."

It's almost disarmingly simple isn't it?

I've been using this approach for several years in my presentation coaching with clients, although it can be used in a number of different contexts. (I understand it's now an approach that's been adopted by some schools.) My goal is to be specific and clear in my feedback and having the above phrases helps me achieve this objective by focusing on what I'm going to say. If someone has several areas they need to improve that's fine. By using this approach the emphasis is on improvement, not criticism.

You can also ask people to reflect themselves on "what worked well" followed by "even better if . . . ?" You're giving people a simple framework in which to focus their answers. Just remember though, not everyone has the necessary knowledge or awareness to answer these questions thoroughly or to everyone's satisfaction.

So the emphasis is primarily on ***you*** giving feedback rather than trying to tease out the information from someone. Trust me; I've seen managers try the latter approach. It can be painful to watch. And time consuming.

Bite Size Wisdom

> We've sacrificed a lot in our quest to protect people's feelings by deluging them with diplomacy

I wonder if for everyone's sake we could just simply cut to the chase and get to the point. And that's exactly what we can do by using the "What worked well" and "Even better if . . ." approach.

When you do, remember the gloves are not off and be aware of the positive and negative impact of your words. Cutting to the chase is fine, telling someone they have the potential not to be crap isn't.

So after you've given your feedback you might also want to ask if they have any comments or questions about what you've said. Your points may need clarifying and if someone disagrees with your comments welcome this as an opportunity to discuss things further. You could end your feedback session by asking the person two further questions:

1. **What have you learnt from this experience?**
2. **What, if anything, would you do differently next time?**

Take the above approach with people and you've potentially motivated them to move on. You've made your criticism count, not crucify.

Bite Size Challenge

Identify a situation when you can use the phrases "What worked well" and "Even better if . . ."

There are of course some situations that arise where such an approach is not appropriate. Perhaps there's been a breach in health and safety or a major mistake has occurred at work leading to a loss in business or an extremely unhappy customer. Remember, even in such cases the emphasis is on fixing problems, not fixing the blame and destroying someone's confidence. To help you do so the following questions will help:

1. **How did that happen?**
2. **Why did that happen?**
3. **What needs to be done now to resolve the issue?**

Make sure you spend as much time on question three as you do on the first two. Avoid getting bogged down in the causes and make sure there's sufficient time given to solutions. This approach ensures people are motivated to improve and equipped to avoid a repeat of the same mistake.

Bite Size Challenge

Who in your organization needs support in how they give feedback to others?

Work out why they're whinging

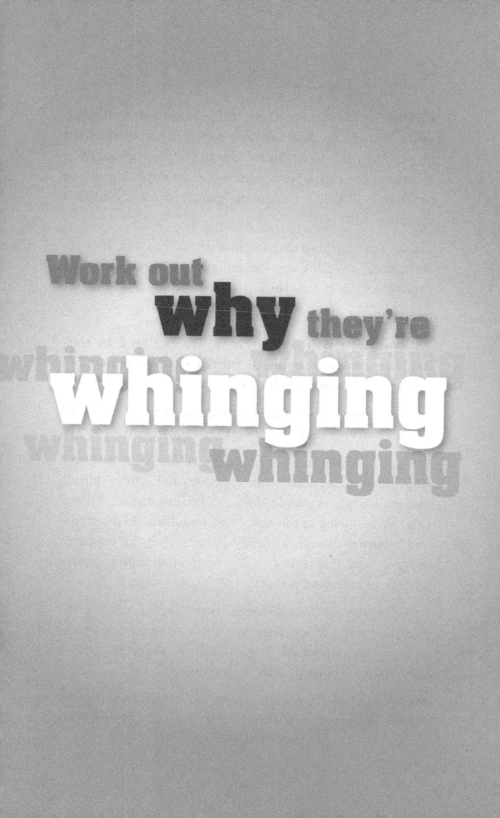

There's a lot to moan about in the world at the moment. Although to be fair, whatever period of history you lived in, people would always find things to complain about. Even Adam and Eve clearly weren't happy about not being able to eat from a particular tree in the garden of Eden. And that didn't end well.

But here's something that might surprise you. Whether it's changes at work, the cost of living, or concerns about the climate, negativity is normal.

In fact, it might even be necessary.

An over-optimistic approach to life can lead to self-delusion and not prepare us for the challenges that life will inevitably present us with.

So the real issue is not whether people are negative but what's caused them to be so and how long they'll stay in such a mindset.

You see, I actually think negative people can get a hard time from others. Many motivational speakers and authors ridicule and mock negative people. They can become caricatured and perceived as being at the root of all problems. Their attitude and behaviour is seen as firmly slamming on the brakes to progress and they can actually be treated with a certain amount of scorn and disdain.

I confess I've probably joined in such "neg bashing" in the past. I've worn my positivity with pride and looked upon the so-called unenlightened "neg heads" or "whingers" with a certain degree of patronizing sympathy.

I've felt justified in doing so. In many ways it can be quite good fun coming up with new labels to describe our negative friends and colleagues. Two of my favourites are "mood hoovers" and "B.M.W.s" – people who Bitch, Moan and Whinge. Such terms never fail to raise a smile from my audiences and colleagues. Using them is almost a guarantee of a cheap laugh. And such comments can be valid and describe very succinctly the behaviour of some people.

But I have my concerns.

Bite Size Wisdom

> Giving people labels can be amusing, but they can also be limiting

Negative people and negative behaviour can be easily dismissed. Disregarded. Swept under the carpet.

But are we being too dismissive?

Ever considered that there may be genuine reasons for some people's concerns?

Rather than ostracize such people and ignore their behaviour we might well benefit from trying to understand what are the underlying reasons and causes for it. Rather than just respond to "what we see," a more effective approach might be to try and uncover and understand "what you don't see."

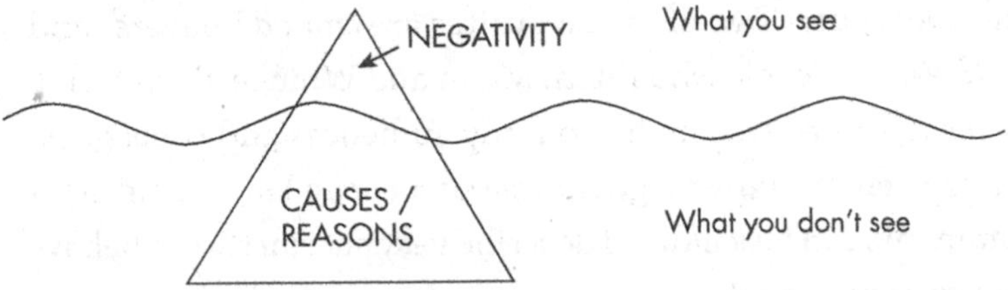

Let me be clear. I'm not suggesting that negativity should now be enthusiastically embraced and encouraged and we start each day thinking and discussing all we have to feel negative about. (You can watch the news if you want to do that.)

But I am saying let's be less dismissive of people's negativity and rather than see it as a trait that needs to be quashed immediately, let's spend some time seeking to identify and understand why people are thinking and behaving in such a way.

There will be many reasons. Let's consider three to get us started.

1. Some people are miserable by nature

It's fair to say that some people you encounter in life wear their coat of negativity like it's an old long lost friend. It's comfortable. It seems to suit them. It's almost as if, if there is a God who's at the heart of creation, he or she has designated that a certain percentage of the population will have a negative or pessimistic outlook on life. Period.

Perhaps there's just very little some people can do to counteract their negative tendencies. Perhaps they've been wired this way to give the "positives" someone to poke fun at, or it's nature's way of making sure there's some form of natural balance to the positive people.

Perhaps negative people's primary function on this planet is to assist positive people in keeping their feet on the ground and not getting too carried away with their ideas.

OK, I admit the above is written slightly tongue in cheek, but it does seem to be the case that some people's nature means they're wired to see the glass half empty. (I've come across some people who are so negative they haven't even got a glass.)

Will they ever change?

Possibly not.

But they can learn to become more aware of how their negative outlook can impact them and those around them and learn to manage it.

They may never become naturally optimistic. Positivity will never be their default position, but you can help them to focus more on the positives and the possibilities and not solely focus on the negatives.

Here's another possible reason for people's negativity.

2. A lack of self-confidence

People's negativity could in many ways be a misdiagnosed and slightly confused cry for help. Perhaps they don't feel very confident about themselves or a particular situation that they find themselves in, but rather than admit the fact (which to be fair might not always be easy to do) it is expressed in negative comments or a negative outlook. People may well look for reasons to justify their lack of confidence which in turn blinds them to the positives that also exist.

If a lack of confidence is someone's main reason for their negativity then some coaching, support and encouragement from someone else will be the required antidote and hopefully reveal that their negativity is more of a temporary condition rather than a permanent character trait.

This might not be the case simply in the workplace but, if you have children, also at home. A child's negative approach to a subject at school could be down to the fact that they don't believe they are very good at it and struggle as a result. Although some subjects may be perceived as simply boring, perhaps another reason for their negativity could be due to their lack of confidence. Some focused help in this area might not completely alleviate their negativity, but it might help.

Also be aware that for some people the lack of confidence that fuels their negativity stems from the fact they're doing something they don't enjoy or feel incapable of doing well. Remember, a fundamental human need is to feel confident in what we do.

Bite Size Wisdom

> Teaching a pig to sing is not only hard work – its demoralizing for all concerned

So, where possible, playing to people's strengths should see an uplift in confidence and in their attitude.

Here's a third possible reason.

3. A perceived sense of injustice

Sometimes people's negativity is simply a label bestowed upon them because they have failed to embrace a particular action or outlook. An unwillingness to do so is simply dismissed as a negative or resistant attitude.

Well, part of that response may be due to a person's pessimistic nature or a possible cry for help, but equally it could be simply down to the fact that they don't agree with a decision or the reasons behind it. Rather than dismissing someone's negativity, which could further stiffen their resistance and deepen their resentment, at least try and appreciate where they're coming from.

Involve people in understanding the process in coming to a particular decision or outlook. Explain to them why this might not be an ideal solution but the reasons why under the circumstances this may be the most realistic way forward. Point out, if appropriate, the dangers of maintaining the status quo. Remaining there may feel comfortable in the short term, but could be dangerous in the long term.

Some decisions I appreciate are not open to debate and discussion. Quick decisive actions are on occasions the order of the day. But that doesn't have to be the case all the time.

Bite Size Wisdom

Rather than resent people's resistance, take time out to understand the reasons for it

Whilst it's unhealthy and unnecessary to analyze and justify every decision you make to people (although some organizations have been notorious for doing just that) the steamroller approach to communication is not our only other option. **If you want to engage and win round people with a negative outlook, recognize their perspective could be valid. What they require from you above all is not necessarily a reversal of your decision and for you to agree with them, but an acknowledgement and appreciation of where they're coming from.**

Once you've done this it's likely that there'll be more cooperation and less time wasted on unproductive stand-offs.

Deep down most people want to be happy, not miserable. So your goal is to help people identify the reasons for their negativity and to help them through it. Look out for ideas in the next three chapters to help you do just that, whilst remembering the lessons from an earlier chapter – that some people are lightbulbs. They don't want to change, no matter how much you want to help them. Equally reflect on this point: Perhaps the main underlying reason for a person's negativity is down to how they're managed.

Bite Size Challenge

Identify a person whose levels of negativity and pessimism seem above average to you. What do you think are the main reasons behind their negativity? What can you do to challenge or support them?

How to make people feel S.P.E.C.I.A.L.

PART I

I wonder if you've ever thought about the following: What's the real issue as to why people fall out with each other?

You see, behind all the gossip, the gory details and the fallout from our conflict with others lies a very important and often overlooked fact. The heart of the issue for many people was simply this:

> *"I didn't feel important."*

People might not even be aware this is the reason and they're unlikely to articulate their feelings in such a clear way. But. . .

Bite Size Wisdom

> When you peel back the layers of frustration and hurt that often lead to anger you'll invariably find someone who doesn't feel valued or important

It may have been triggered in many different ways: feeling ignored, lied to, ridiculed, overlooked, not listened to, not consulted, or being taken for granted. The reasons may be many but the impact is the same.

So in this chapter and the next we're going to look. at seven ways to ensure that people do feel valued and important. Because when they do they're going to be much easier to communicate and deal with. Applying these ideas will not only reduce the amount of conflict you experience but also increase the quality and depth of relationship you have with others, both in and outside the workplace.

To help us achieve such an outcome we're going to use the acronym S.P.E.C.I.A.L. to help us remember each of the seven points.

Here's what each letter stands for:

S erve

P ersonalized

E ncourage

C ourtesy

I nterest

A ppreciation

L isten

Now let's look at each point in detail.

1. Serve

An interesting word that for some people might conjure up associations more with a servant, or someone who works in a restaurant or retail outlet. It's probably not the first word on people's list of strategies to engage, influence and motivate others.

I'm suggesting it should be.

It should be something that becomes core to our character and at the heart of our attitude when we're dealing with others.

Having such an attitude of wanting to serve may have prevented my rather uncomfortable experience with Mark, whom we encountered in the earlier chapter "Check out your attitude."

You see, rather than believe that the world revolves solely around us and the only way to achieving happiness is to do all we can to get our goals met, we should in fact look at what we can do to meet the needs and goals of others. As the American motivational speaker Zig Ziglar says:

Bite Size Wisdom

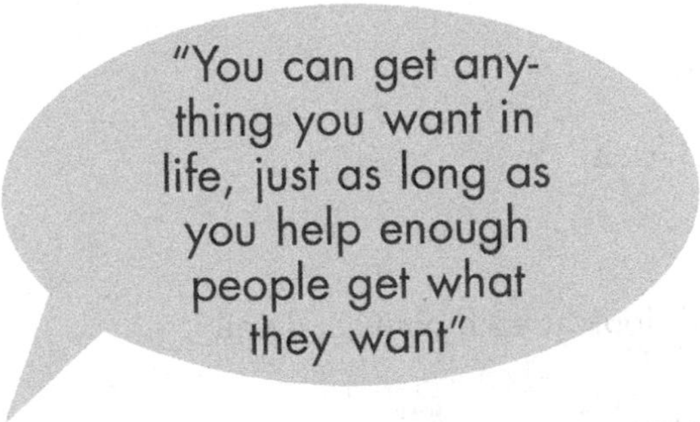
"You can get anything you want in life, just as long as you help enough people get what they want"

As a professional speaker I regularly remind myself that my primary goal is to serve my audience. Of course I want to do a great job and be appreciated for what I do – I'd be lying if I said any different. But my main focus should not be

"What do people think of me?"

but rather

"What can I do to help meet my audience's needs?"

This automatically means I become more outward and less inward-focused. Ultimately, my success comes from helping my audience. And a by-product of meeting their needs is that there's a good chance my own needs will be met too.

When an organization's main focus is how can we meet and ultimately exceed our customers' needs they're far more likely to be successful. When leaders ask "How can we best serve our staff to assist them in doing the best job possible?" they're putting service at the heart of their culture.

Now, how you "serve" others specifically will depend on the person and the context. I'm not suggesting that after you've cooked a meal for a loved one you follow up with "Did everything meet with your expectations and what can we do to improve your experience next time?" followed by a questionnaire which on completion will be entered into a prize draw to win a free weekend in Whitby. Neither are you there to meet the every need of your children, although that probably will be the case at least in their first 18 months. (Notice I said months, not years.)

But you get my drift. Serving others is an attitude from which our behaviour flows.

So, what does serving look like in practice? Well, practical ways in which we can serve others will be revealed as we continue to look at how we can make others feel S.P.E.C.I.A.L.

2. Personalized

Go on, admit it, which would you prefer – a gift voucher or a present that has clearly been bought with you in mind? A valentine card with your name on it, or one that says "To whom it may concern"?

Get my point?

Make people feel special and important by personalizing your encounters with them.

In business you might well use customers' names when talking with them. I'm made to feel special when I'm working in a particular hotel I use regularly. They reserve a parking space for me with my name on it. Before I've even walked into the hotel I'm already feeling important.

My friend Mark Mitchell runs three car dealerships in the North West of England. He appears to have an obsession with doing all he and his hundred-plus staff can do to make his customers feel special. Letters to customers often include a personalized note at the end from Mark. If he comes across an article that he thinks may be of interest to you he sends you a copy. It seems to be part of his DNA, but it's also good for business, judging by the loyalty of his customers.

There's no guarantee that if you make people feel special by making your encounters with them more personal they'll continue to do business with you. But you've certainly increased the chances.

With loved ones, rather than show your generosity with a cheque or voucher, perhaps a more personalized gift that required some thought on your part will have far greater impact.

Agree?

That's why the phrase "It's the thought that counts" is so true. Showing you've thought about someone even in only a small way can have a huge impact.

Bite Size Wisdom

> Treating someone in a way that is unique to them is a powerful way to make that person feel important

In terms of my own life, what does my wife appreciate – a diamond ring or a packet of midget gems? It's midget gems every time. Lots of people show their love by buying jewellery but my wife knows when I've bought her midget gems I've personalized my gift and given it some thought.

(OK, I've just shown my wife that last paragraph and she informs me that her ideal scenario would be a diamond inside a midget gem – but you know what I mean.)

Make it personal. Treat people as unique individuals with their own particular likes and dislikes and not just one of the crowd. And remember the point we made earlier in the chapter "Treat people as they want to be treated."

Bite Size Challenge

What one thing could you do this week for someone that actually demonstrates you've thought of them personally?

3. Encourage

I've been on this planet a long time. I've encountered hundreds of thousands of people on my travels, either meeting them personally or addressing them in an audience. To date I've spoken in over 40 countries. No one, but no one, has ever said the following:

> *"You know my problem? I've had too much encouragement."*

Now admittedly, give me too much encouragement too often and it begins to lose its impact. But we all need encouragement sometimes.

My friend Lynda describes herself as my CEO – Chief Encouragement Officer. We hardly see each other and rarely talk, but she still lives up to her title with her encouraging messages on social media.

The word encourage literally means "to give courage." That might mean the courage to start something, the courage not to quit or the courage to aim higher. It could also mean that your encouragement gives people the confidence to stop something that clearly isn't working. But rather than feel a failure, your words mean they've learnt from the experience and are better equipped for their next challenge.

Bite Size Wisdom

In a world of setbacks, disappointments and people who are quick to criticize and pull you down, we all need the oxygen of encouragement

Your encouragement might be written on a card, a text, an email or a letter. It might simply be spoken. It doesn't even have to be long.

But words are powerful.

They have the ability to build up or bring down.

Throughout my life there have been countless people who've encouraged me. I remember how my friends Tom Palmer and Paul Sandham's comments had a profound impact on me on one particular occasion. Having seen my proposal for my

SUMO book rejected by one of the top publishers in the UK their advice was simple: "Don't give up. Keep trying. Push more doors." Their words were exactly what I needed to hear, particularly after several setbacks. And after thirteen rejections, I finally received an offer from a publisher.

There might not be any immediate tangible payback to you in encouraging others. There doesn't need to be.

But wouldn't it be great to look back on your life and realize that as a result of your words some people gained the courage to persevere or to aim higher? And the fact that you took the time to encourage them made them feel good enough about themselves to take the next step.

Well guess what?

You can.

Bite Size Challenge

Who in your world needs some encouragement? What can you do to make sure that happens?

How to make people feel S.P.E.C.I.A.L.

PART 2

So far we've looked at three ways to make people feel S.P.E.C.I.A.L. – Serve, Personalize and Encourage. Now let's look at four more ways. Remember, in doing so we're aiming to improve our chances of being able to influence, engage and motivate others whilst at the same time reducing the chances of conflict. Here's the fourth way.

4. Courtesy

The word "respect" is talked about a lot these days. There was even a political party in the UK that went by that name. It's also a term that's become widespread in the sports arena, particularly within football. However, despite its increased usage I'm not sure if people even know exactly how to show respect to others.

Well here's a start. Show some courtesy.

Courtesy may seem an old fashioned word in today's modern society, but it lies at the heart of showing respect for others.

Never underestimate how positive the impact of using the words "please" and "thank you" can be on others. Or let me put it another way. Try being rude and discourteous to people and see how helpful and cooperative they become.

And courtesy shouldn't be used sparingly as if it's a rare and limited commodity or shown only to those you consider important.

Neither should it be reserved solely for those who have in some way earned the right to be treated with respect.

Bite Size Wisdom

> Having respect for others should be our starting point in a relationship. Not a possible destination

Showing courtesy for others is a behaviour that is hopefully taught in schools, and needs to be modelled by parents and the wider community. It's something I aim to do consistently with the people I lead in my SUMO team. You see, talking down to people and treating them rudely is another way of saying "you're not important, you're not my equal." Everyone, whatever their creed, colour, sexual orientation or history, deserves some courtesy and respect.

And courtesy is not just a simple case of saying "please" and "thank you." It's about thinking of other people's needs as well as your own. It's about replying to emails when you said you would. It's about returning someone's phone call like you promised to. It's about doing all you can to be on time for a meeting or event rather than drifting in when it suits you. And this is a big one. It's also about choosing not to check a new message on your phone during a conversation with someone, unless you've apologized for the need to do so.

Simple stuff?

Absolutely.

Obvious advice?

Probably.

And yet having been in business for over 30 years I still experience a lack of courtesy from people on an almost daily basis – fuelled in the main by a combination of ignorance and busyness.

But that's no excuse.

Bite Size Wisdom

No one ever feels important when you keep checking your phone whilst they're still talking

Yet when we do show courtesy, even in only small ways, it all adds to the intangible mix of positive behaviours that develop our likeability. And when we're liked by others we're in a much better position to be able to influence them. **People are more likely to be open to our ideas when they're open to us as people.**

There are no guarantees of course, but you do increase your chances of engaging more effectively with others. Now, I appreciate someone like Steve Jobs achieved outstanding success without always demonstrating this particular trait – in fact he had a reputation for being rude and discourteous with many people. And I realize there will be others like him. But I hope, generally speaking, such behaviour should be seen as the exception rather than the rule.

Agree?

Bite Size Challenge

- In what way may your behaviour be seen as discourteous to others?
- How courteous would your close friends and colleagues say you are?

5. Interest

Here's another obvious but often overlooked way in which to develop better relationships with the people you live and work with.

Be interested in people.

Stop obsessing about your own world and your own needs all the time. Show interest in what's going on in the world of other people.

Maybe just a simple question such as "Any plans for the weekend?" or if you're meeting for the first time, "Where's that accent from?"

Trust me. If you want to influence other people start by showing a *genuine* interest in them. But remember, if you're faking interest people will notice.

A sales assistant recently asked me if I had any plans for the rest of the day. I was pleasantly surprised by his interest and told him I was off later that day with my family to see the comedian Michael McIntyre.

His response?

Looking down at the items I'd just purchased he asked "Would you like a bag for those?"

My immediate thoughts?

"Hey pal, I wish you'd never shown any supposed interest in me in the first place. You've totally ruined the impact of your question by ignoring my answer. Rather than make me feel important you've now succeeded in hacking me off. And you've managed to do so in almost record time. Congratulations."

OK, maybe I was having a bad day, but you get my point don't you?

Bite Size Wisdom

> If you're going to ask a question, be prepared to listen to the answer

So, if you want to connect with people remember to show some interest in their world and ideally don't just listen but also try and remember some salient points of what they've said. Even if it's just one or two headlines.

Why's that important?

Well, what a great way to make an impression on someone next time you meet if you ask a question about something they talked about previously. So few people do this that you're bound to stand out from the crowd when you do.

Isn't this worth trying with at least one person you meet this week?

6. Appreciation

Let me remind you of a quote I shared in an earlier chapter from the author Philip Yancey: "The opposite of love is not hate – it's indifference."

I find that very challenging. Perhaps at times without even realizing it we can start to take our colleagues, customers or loved ones for granted. Complacency can creep up on us and if we're not careful our attitude towards others can slowly turn to indifference. Familiarity can breed apathy.

The antidote?

There are a number. Some of which we've explored previously, particularly in the chapter "No investment, no return."

Here's another.

Start showing that you do value the people around you and show some appreciation. Make appreciating others part of your core values and not an add-on to your to-do list if you get time.

Put some thought into it. Write a note. Send a text (although not when you're in the middle of a conversation with someone else). Make a call. Send a gift. Spring a surprise. Go the extra mile for a birthday or anniversary. How you do it is up to you, just make sure you do it.

You see, the very act of thinking about how you can show appreciation to others will in itself help arrest the advance of indifference.

With each of my clients I send a thank you card after I've worked with them. I never want to take their business for granted. I'm thankful for the opportunity they've given me. It's not a costly exercise and it takes minutes rather than hours to do. But it's now become a habit, and showing appreciation to others is not a bad habit to develop. And it's not just something to practise at work. It's equally important to show appreciation in your personal life.

My son Matt is a doctor. But aged 15 he wasn't sure what he wanted to do as a career. Then his Biology teacher left and Mrs Shaw arrived as their replacement. She totally engaged Matt in the subject. So much so that that was the turning point in him deciding he wanted to be a doctor.

I wrote to Mrs Shaw to thank her for the impact she'd had on Matt. I told her she was M.A.D. – Making A Difference. In her reply she wrote "Thanks for letting me know. You made my year."

I hope showing Mrs Shaw some appreciation helps to continue to motivate her in her work, and reminded her of the positive influence she and other teachers can have on young people's lives.

Bite Size Challenge

Your mission for today, should you choose to accept it, is to show appreciation to someone in whatever creative way you choose. Feel free to share what you did and the impact it made by telling me about it. You can email me at Contact@theSUMOguy.com – I promise to personally acknowledge each email.

7. Listen

Have you ever been talking to someone and it's become obvious they're no longer listening? How did that make you feel?

Now contrast that with the time when you really felt you were being listened to by someone.

It felt good didn't it?

Listening is perhaps a bigger subject than most of us are aware of. I simply want to put it back on your radar. Here's the reality:

Bite Size Wisdom

Sometimes being a person of influence is knowing when to stop talking and when to start listening

You see, I think we can be captivated by a great speaker, but we're often helped by a great listener.

But remember this. Listening is hard. If you think it's easy you're clearly not very good at it.

There are many challenges to doing it well. Thoughts pop into your head unannounced, sometimes triggered by what you've just heard. It's easy to be distracted.

Be aware that your prejudices inform your thinking, so it's difficult not to judge what you're hearing and be quick to offer your advice or opinion. Now that's fine in general conversation. It's to be expected. But it can also hinder you and become a barrier when all the other person wants is to be listened to.

And people rarely tell you the whole story. They miss stuff out. Leave gaps. If you don't listen well and don't ask questions you're not getting the whole picture. That can lead to problems.

To listen really well our attitude and starting point should be ***"tell me more"*** rather than ***"here's what I think."*** Remember, sometimes it's not about "us," it's about "them." If you want people to open up, to tell you more, to get to the heart of the issue you need to listen.

Develop "the gift of the gap." Yes, that's right, "gap," not "gab." Allow people space. Don't feel the need to fill every silence. Gaps in conversation are OK. They allow the other person time to clarify and articulate their thoughts.

If I'm angry, listen. If I'm upset, listen.

If I'm excited, listen. If I'm gutted, listen.

Sometimes I don't always want or need a solution. Sometimes I'm not after an opinion.

Sometimes I just need to be heard. To be understood. To be listened to.

Bite Size Wisdom

> Some people need to tell you their story before they're ready to hear your solution

Perhaps then and only then do I feel ready to explore a way forward, and to listen to your perspective. You see, when I don't feel I've been listened to I'm less likely to be receptive to your thoughts and ideas. Your words wash over me.

Remember, I need to feel important. I need to feel understood. And perhaps the most effective way of helping to achieve both is to listen to me.

So will you?

Or will you just wait until it's your turn to talk?

Bite Size Challenge

Who do you know who needs a good listening to today?

So that's the final approach of how to make people feel S.P.E.C.I.A.L. Over the last two chapters we've explored seven ways to do that. Before we go on to our next chapter let's just remind ourselves of the seven again. As we do so which one in particular stands out for you? Serve, Personalized, Encourage, Courtesy, Interest, Appreciation and Listen.

How to pick people up when they're feeling down

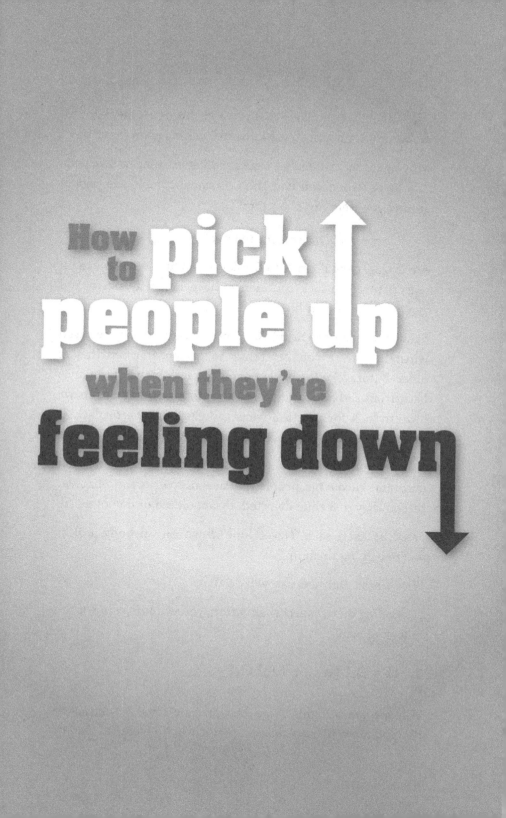

Although it's unlikely that you and I have ever met I do feel fairly confident that I know something about your past.

My guess is that when you were a toddler learning to take your first steps, when you had the occasional tumble the people around you were not shouting:

"Loser – you'll never learn to walk."

Am I right? (And if I'm not I think I've just uncovered the main reason why you lack confidence, have low self-esteem and avoid taking risks in life.)

Sadly, for many people all that encouragement they received when they were younger tends to disappear when they're older. But if we're to enable people to reach higher, to bounce back from setbacks and to achieve their potential, then we have to look for practical ways to help them, particularly if they've had a few falls recently.

So we're going to explore what you can do to positively influence and encourage people, particularly when for whatever reason they're feeling dejected, disappointed or demoralized.

Jesse Jackson said "Never look down on anybody, unless you're helping them up."

Wise words. But how can you do that?

Depending on the specific situation, you will find some of the following help:

1. It's OK to not feel OK

Help people recognize that certain emotional responses to disappointments or setbacks are normal. To feel mad, bad or sad is OK. It's not wrong to feel that way. Actually, it's a sign that they care.

That's a good thing.

But there is a danger. People can stay "wallowing" in such emotions for too long. And that can lead to them making irrational judgements about themselves and others when emotionally low.

That's a dangerous thing.

So help people to understand that how they're feeling emotionally is normal, but also temporary. Like the sunshine in the north of England it will be experienced from time to time, but it's never going to become a permanent feature of the weather landscape. Once you've given people some time and space, consider which of the following points could be of help to them.

2. Reframe failure

Let's be clear about what it means to fail. Firstly, failing isn't final. Neither does failing make someone a failure.

Just as falling is part of the process in learning how to walk, failing is part of the journey in learning, growing and succeeding. When people fail they're in effect receiving feedback. Maybe they need to adjust their approach, try a different strategy or practise more. It's not a permanent slight on their character.

Unfortunately, so much emotional baggage has become attached to the word "failure," that we need to remind people that anyone who has ever led a meaningful life has at some time failed.

So when people experience a setback acknowledge their disappointment and then help them to see it as helpful feedback for next time. It's part of their learning journey. It's not the end of it.

To help people do this use the two questions we explored earlier: "What can you learn from this?" and "What would you do differently next time?" By doing so you're helping people to focus on their future, not their failure.

Bite Size Wisdom

Failure isn't final
until you stop trying

3. Look for the positives

Setbacks and disappointments can grossly distort our perspective on reality. If you want to help people at such times remember to point out the positives. Be careful when and how you do this though, as it can sometimes be perceived as patronizing and possibly insensitive.

So I'm not suggesting if a friend has lost their legs in an accident that you march in breezily to their hospital ward whistling "Always look on the bright side of life" or state "Oh well, at least you've still got your arms." Depending on the situation tact and diplomacy may be required. And you also have to choose the right time. Pointing out the positives too soon could be both hurtful and unhelpful. (Please, under no circumstances, when you're with a friend who has recently experienced a break-up, say "Oh well, there's plenty more fish in the sea.")

One of the most effective ways to support someone is to ask questions that help them identify for themselves some positives in a situation.

Questions such as:

- **"What did go well in your presentation?"**
- **"Which part of the exam did you feel you did well on?"**
- **"Think of a time when you did handle that situation well. What was happening then?"**
- **"What are the positives you can take from the experience? How can we build on them?"**
- **"What are some of the things that are going well in your life at the moment?"**

Looking for positives when someone is feeling particularly low does not come naturally for many people. It's not a typical default response. Therefore, people need to be both challenged and reminded in a supportive way that invariably it's not all bad news. **However, make sure you do so without dismissing their pain or underestimating their level of disappointment.**

4. Go for quick wins

How do you help people who are feeling demotivated? Simply remember the following:

Bite Size Wisdom

Nothing motivates like success

As Thomas Carlyle said, **"Nothing builds a sense of confidence and self-esteem like accomplishment."**

So, some form of success, no matter how small, can help fuel hope. That's crucial because it can breed confidence. It helps people to "move on" in a more motivated way, because people begin to believe they're capable of achieving success.

A great question to prevent people wallowing for too long is to ask **"Right, what needs to happen now?"** or **"What's the one action we can take now that will indicate we're moving in the right direction?"**

Make sure you make a note of those questions. They really will help you to help others.

When I talk about the importance of quick wins I'm speaking from experience.

Let me explain.

I'm probably best known for a book I wrote in 2005, *SUMO (Shut Up, Move On)*. As I mentioned earlier, it was rejected by 13 publishers. Each rejection came as a personal blow to my confidence. I actually received four negative replies on the same day. Boy, was that a great morning!

But a quick win for me was to feel by the end of the day I'd taken some action towards getting my book published. That meant either tweaking my initial proposal (at one stage I actually considered dropping the phrase SUMO from the title) or contacting another publisher.

With one publisher who'd rejected my manuscript I still convinced them to meet me personally to discuss my book idea in more detail. They still rejected it, but the fact that they'd agreed to meet me felt like a small win. It fuelled my motivation and provided some momentum.

Now this next point is really important.

What I've discovered over time is that right feelings follow right actions.

By going for quick wins I am taking back some control and making some progress.

My motivation actually comes as a result of my action, not the other way round.

So in terms of helping ourselves and others to keep on keeping on, this next piece of wisdom is vital to remember.

Bite Size Wisdom

> Focus on progress, not perfection

It's not reaching the perfect score of 10 that counts to begin with. It's simply focusing on what actions are needed to help people get closer to 10. That means if someone is currently on "two" your aim is to help them to reach for three or four.

Yes, reaching "ten" may still seem far off but it's closer now than it was at the beginning of the process. So celebrate progress. Such an approach encourages people to persevere and not to become daunted by what they still need to achieve.

Remind people that success is ultimately an accumulation of small victories, and that's why achieving some quick wins can be vital in helping lift the spirits of people who are currently feeling demotivated or demoralized.

Bite Size Challenge

What quick wins could you identify to help your team or someone close to you come back from a setback?

5. Change location

Sometimes a change of environment or location can help stimulate a new perspective. A meeting in a pub or cafe rather than the office may help. Sometimes it might be going into the countryside rather than the city and on occasions maybe even a few days away.

Changing the physical space in which people operate has the potential to create a different outlook, generate new ideas and stimulate a new way of thinking by shaking up our normal routine and exposing us to a different environment.

A change can at times be literally as good as a rest and help provide the space necessary for people to rebuild, recover and re-charge.

As my office is based in our home and I work with my wife, we often benefit from taking some time out by going for a long walk to talk through some issues. On occasions, we will get away for a night and find we gain greater clarity about a problem simply by removing ourselves from our day-to-day work environment and the distractions that brings.

Bite Size Challenge

We've explored five ways to pick people up when they're feeling down:

1. It's OK not to feel OK
2. Reframe failure
3. Look for the positives
4. Go for quick wins
5. Change location

Choose one strategy you can use to help someone when they've experienced a setback or disappointment.

How to talk so people listen

We can all talk. The problem is getting people to listen. Yet if we're going to successfully influence, engage and motivate those around us then it's important we understand what does and doesn't work when we're communicating with them.

Let's start by looking at three common communication mistakes that actually do more to switch people off rather than switch them on to our message. As we do, reflect on which ones you may have been guilty of or have seen others do.

1. Drowning people in detail

Almost everywhere I go I come across people who think the best way to convince and persuade people over a particular argument is to tell them everything they know on the subject. They mistakenly believe "If I bombard you with enough facts you're bound to submit to my way of thinking."

Wrong.

Bite Size Wisdom

> People who are drowning in detail are usually gasping for insight

People are seeking clarity amidst the clutter of information being spewed out at them. But if they don't seem to be persuaded by what is being said, what do some people do?

Give you even more detail.

They press on regardless and ignore the tell-tale signs that they're losing their audience. People may be physically present in a conversation or meeting, but their mind is often somewhere else.

The biggest clue that this is happening is usually in their eyes. They glaze over. The lights are on but no one's at home. The wheel's turning but the hamster's dead.

Another, perhaps less subtle, clue that people have had enough of you talking is when they bang their head on a desk or start using matchsticks to keep their eyes open. Hey, even people with Self Awareness Deficiency Syndrome might pick up on these cues, although there's always someone who, despite your behaviour being strange, will press on regardless.

Bite Size Wisdom

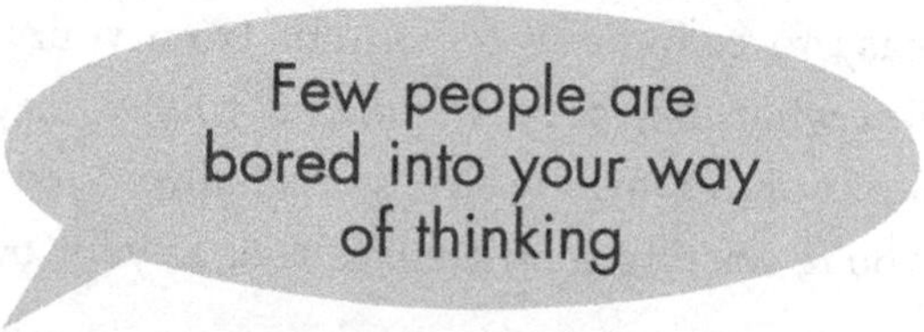

Few people are bored into your way of thinking

The reality is most presentations and meetings would benefit by being reduced in time by 50%.

And the harsh truth is that the applause some presenters receive at the end of their talk is not a sign of appreciation. It's an expression of relief.

It's also worth realizing that when you utter the words "to cut a long story short" most of your listeners are inwardly giving you a standing ovation and praying that you do.

So here's the deal. Brevity is best.

If people want more detail they'll generally ask for it. In fact you can always prompt them by saying, "That's an overview, does that cover what you need at the moment or would you like me to go into more detail about a particular area?"

In day-to-day communication perhaps in a more informal context the same principle still applies. Unless it's crucial for the other person to be aware of the full facts or it's a particularly exciting or humorous story then be content to just give the highlights, unless people ask for more. Even then make sure it's extended highlights and not a complete re-run of events.

2. Failing to make your message relevant to your audience

It's so easy to communicate content from your perspective alone. But what may seem important to you may have very little relevance to someone else, and a failure to recognize this means you're wasting their time as well as your own.

Too many people start from the perspective "What do I want to say?" rather than "What does my audience need to hear?"

It's crucial we wake up to the fact that people will switch off unless your message is easy to understand, and, most importantly, has some relevance to their own lives. Otherwise, what is the point of you talking?

3. Focusing on facts and forgetting the feelings

People aren't only interested and engaged by what you say but also by the way you say it. Appealing to people's intellect alone will rarely bring about change in them. You need to engage their emotions as well.

Bite Size Wisdom

When you want to persuade people, appeal to the heart, not just the head

So you'll need to give some attention to how you'll deliver your message and not concentrate solely on the content. That means thinking of ways to make your message more engaging and to consider what stories or anecdotes you can use to illustrate what you have to say. **Remember Martin Luther King Junior didn't inspire a generation with the phrase "I have a strategic plan."** He had a dream. He did focus on facts, but he also stirred people's feelings.

Too few people realize the importance of doing both.

Here's a recap of those mistakes:

1. Drowning people in detail.
2. Failing to make your message relevant to your audience.
3. Focusing on facts and forgetting the feelings.

Which ones have you experienced or perhaps been guilty of?

OK, so that's the problem. What's the solution? Well try these five ideas for starters.

1. Recognize their reality

Take time to think about other people's needs and concerns. Subconsciously many people, when you talk to them about a particular subject, are asking themselves "Why should I care?"

Think about where people might be struggling, or what problem your message might be the solution to. Tailor your message so that you scratch where people are itching. Because if you don't you'll have a polite audience but not one that's proactively engaged in wanting to hear what you have to say.

Prepare your content by keeping in mind that phrase in your audience's mind – "Why should I care?" And ask yourself "How can I make my message relevant to my audience?"

2. Remember the 90/90 rule

I can't prove this scientifically but potentially 90% of the impression you make on an audience has been achieved within the first 90 seconds of you communicating with them. And although all of your message will be important it's crucial that in those opening moments you grab people's attention.

Here are some examples of how you could do this.

- Start in a very clear and direct way:

  "I'm here to discuss the number one fear in most people's lives and how one simple idea can help you overcome it."

- You could start with a rhetorical question which by its very nature immediately engages your audience:

  "If you had to give someone just one piece of advice that you wish you'd received when you were younger, what would it be?"

- Perhaps you start with a story or spell out very clearly in what way they will benefit from listening to what you have to say.

Bite Size Wisdom

> Inside 90 seconds you could already have people wishing they were somewhere else, or engrossed and curious as to what you'll say next

So make sure you make those first 90 seconds count.

3. Begin with the end in mind

This point is actually the second habit from Dr Stephen Covey's book 7 *Habits of Highly Effective People* (Simon and Schuster Ltd, 2004). It's a great approach to have and applies in life generally and to communication specifically.

It boils down to this. Are you totally clear on the purpose of your presentation, your meeting or your conversation?

To help you further, can you fill in the following blanks *before* you start your communication?

As a result of today's presentation/meeting/conversation the following will have been achieved:

Bite Size Wisdom

Take people on a clear journey. Not on a magical mystery tour

Remember, if you're not totally clear in your mind about the purpose and direction of your communication why on earth would you expect your audience to be?

Here's another great way to clarify things in your own mind.

Ask yourself what do you want people to *know*, *feel* and *do* after your presentation, meeting or conversation has finished?

Focus on these outcomes *before* you start preparing the detail, content and structure of what you're going to say.

Doing so cuts the clutter and provides clarity concerning what it is that is really important. The other additional benefit is that you'll save time. Both yours and your audience's.

Let me end this point with an example of a sign I saw on the centre of a table in the meeting room of one of my clients. It simply said this:

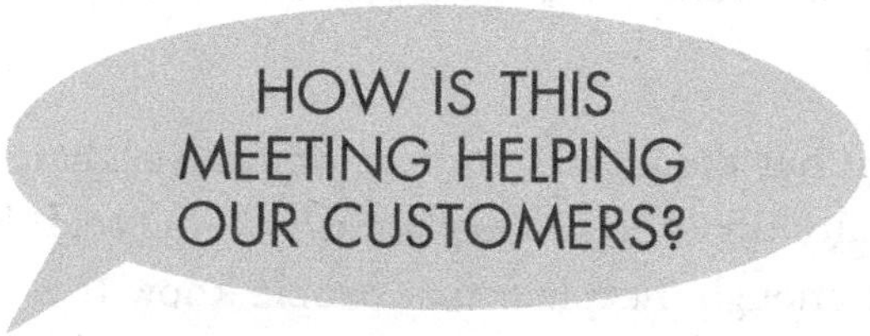
HOW IS THIS
MEETING HELPING
OUR CUSTOMERS?

What a great way of keeping people focused and clear on their ultimate purpose.

4. Point out the pain before providing the prescription

It's not easy for people to enthusiastically buy into a solution when they're not totally convinced there's a problem. In my presentations I often explore seven questions to help you SUMO (Shut Up, Move On). (If you would like an electronic copy, email Contact@theSUMOguy.com.) They're particularly good questions to ask when faced with a challenge. The first one especially often resonates with people:

> *"Where is this issue on a scale of 1 – 10? (Where 10 = death)"*

However, before I share these seven SUMO questions I first of all highlight the "pain" or problem of what I call "Faulty Thinking." This is a type of thinking that hinders both people's perspective and performance.

I tell stories and use examples to illustrate each type of faulty thinking and I ask my audience to discuss which ones they particularly relate to and do they also know people who "suffer" (I use that word deliberately) from these ways of thinking.

I then point out the impact and consequences when we stay stuck in faulty thinking and explain why being told "be positive" is not enough. I explain that people know they need to be positive, but when times are difficult and challenging they want to know how to do it.

What I'm doing with such an approach is taking my audience on a journey. I'm sharing anecdotes and stories with them, which is a powerful way to engage people at an emotional level. I'm making it very clear there is a problem when our thinking is faulty and highlighting the pain that can be caused as a result of that problem. **You see, I don't just want people to understand the problem. I want them to feel it.**

Do you think at this point they're keen to hear a solution?

You bet they are.

It's only then that I present the "prescription" to the pain, by exploring the seven questions. These help to provide a way for my audience to move out of "Faulty Thinking" and move on to what I call "Fruity Thinking," which is a positive and empowering way to deal with challenges.

Bite Size Wisdom

> If you want people to buy into the solution make sure they've felt the pain of the problem

Remember, it's the combination of facts and feelings that causes people to engage with what you say and take action as a result. Don't focus only on communicating facts. Tap into people's feelings – and by pointing out the pain of a problem you do exactly that.

So is that something you could be more conscious of doing in future? You'll have to decide to what extent you point out the pain and how relevant and realistic such an approach would be within your particular context.

Perhaps worth a try though?

5. Invest in yourself

Learning to speak so people listen is easier said than done. Applying the ideas I've suggested and avoiding the mistakes

I've outlined will definitely help. But if you're serious about developing your ability to engage and persuade your audience, whatever the size, then invest in some further training and coaching. Identify a coach you can work with or a course you can attend. Nothing beats the opportunity to practise and receive feedback to help your raise your game. I'm happy to provide details of the organizations and people I recommend. Please email Contact@theSUMOguy.com for more information.

Alternatively check out the website www.TED.com. You'll have an opportunity to watch some of the world's leading experts speak on a variety of subjects. Learn not just from what they say, but also the way they say it.

Bite Size Challenge

So which of the following five strategies do you need to apply so that when you talk people listen?

1. Recognize their reality
2. Remember the 90/90 rule
3. Begin with the end in mind
4. Point out the pain before providing the prescription
5. Invest in yourself

Who else do you know who would benefit from discovering what's in this chapter? What action will you take to ensure they do?

The ball's in your court

We've explored so many ideas and insights on how to succeed with people, but what impact can succeeding with people really have?

Let's find out.

It was 10 January 1995. 4.30 p.m. I sat nervously waiting for Jacqueline's feedback. It had been an exhausting and challenging day.

Over the next two hours she unpacked in detail her thoughts on how the event I ran on her company's behalf had gone.

Those 120 minutes had a profound impact on me. As someone who had only three years earlier been battling the illness M.E. (or Chronic Fatigue Syndrome) I realized that in many ways it was an achievement even to be sitting where I was.

But I wanted more.

I wanted to develop my skills as a speaker and to grow my business. I wanted to achieve a dream not just to speak in the UK but also to audiences around the world.

As I sat listening to Jacqueline in the reception area of a hotel on the outskirts of Manchester I realized that what I was about to hear would either be the catalyst to fulfilling that dream or a wake-up call that I needed to dump my delusions and start thinking of a plan B.

September 1974. 8.45 a.m. I walk into Mr Jeacock's classroom. I'm about to start my final year in primary school. My family have moved around a lot. It's my fourth different school. I'm ten years old.

My mum is passionate for me to succeed in life but academically I'm comfortably below average. Maths is confusing, science a complete mystery, and I get lost studying geography. I just wish I could quit education now and go to drama school. It's the only subject I seem to have any ability in.

Ten months later I leave school. I say goodbye to Mr Jeacock. I actually cry. I've loved those ten months. The happiest times I've ever had at school.

I've grown in confidence. Academically I've improved. Science is still a mystery to me though.

July 1986. South East London. It's the middle of the long university holidays. It's actually sunny in England. I've joined 50 or so other people to get involved as a volunteer in some community work for a Christian charity.

We're placed into teams with people who are strangers. Within days we're close friends.

My team leader is a guy called Paul. He's slightly older than me. We click. On the surface we seem to share few common interests though. He fails to understand the offside rule in football. I confess my love affair with Russian literature never even made it to a first date. But we laugh lots. We share a similar view of the world and have a deep fascination for people, and what makes them tick.

Thirty-six years later he's still my best mate. Where I'm at in life today has been largely influenced by him. On one level he's had no impact whatsoever in this book. He's yet to read a single chapter. But the wisdom, insight and experience that he's lavished upon me with a mixture of humour and amazing patience hopefully permeates many of the pages.

18 November 2012. It's Sunday morning. 6.30 a.m. I'm awake early again. I've just binned the final chapter of the first edition of this book.

Not a single word of it remains.

I've decided to write about Jacqueline, Mr Jeacock and my mate Paul instead.

They never needed to read this book. They were already living it.

They have already discovered how to succeed with people.

They're not perfect. They'll still make mistakes and have their challenges like all of us.

But I know the impact they've had on me. In their own different ways they've shaped who I've become.

Mr Jeacock instilled some belief and self-confidence into me. I was ten years old at the time. That's a good age to develop some confidence.

Jacqueline's professionalism and encouragement meant her feedback of my first speaking event in January 1995 did not crucify me. It became the catalyst for my career.

And Paul's ongoing support, despite some of his own personal struggles, means I've had the privilege of having a mentor and role model as well as a mate.

Between them they've shown me the impact succeeding with people can actually have.

It really isn't pink and fluffy stuff. It can be life enhancing. More than that, applying even only a few of the ideas we've explored can be life changing both in our personal and professional lives.

But whether they are or not is down to you.

Your challenge and mine is not acquiring more knowledge. It's not even about coming up with new ideas. It's about doing something with what we know.

It's about realizing that all we've explored so far is easy to do.

It's also easy not to do.

So will this book just be another one to put back on the shelf and leave undisturbed for the next few years? Will some of the ideas and insights you've gained be quickly forgotten?

I hope not.

In fact, I hope you challenge yourself to do something right now. I'm putting the ball in your court and asking you to do something that will probably take less than five minutes.

Get in touch. Message me with your feedback via Instagram or X @theSUMOguy, or email me at Contact@theSUMOguy.com.

All you have to do is tell me one thing that has stood out for you from this book. Then tell me one thing you're going to do as a result of reading it.

You're probably thinking you can't be bothered.

You're probably thinking it doesn't really matter.

You'd be wrong.

It does matter.

I personally read all the feedback I receive. And I reply. But you're doing this for you, not for me. Taking just one small action can prove the catalyst to taking further small actions. It's a quick win and we already know how good those can be for us, right?

Whatever our future contact, I really do hope that in some small way this book has been of help. Life can be quite a rollercoaster at times, particularly when it comes to dealing with people. They can be our greatest source of joy and our greatest source of heartache.

Mr Jeacock is no longer around to read about his legacy to me. Paul and Jacqueline are.

I hope that having shared this journey with me you now feel equipped and inspired to leave your own legacy in people's lives.

The great thing is you can.

You can actually start today if you want to.

The ball's in your court.

One final thing before I go. Here's a brief reminder of some of what we've covered.

I hope it helps.

How to succeed with people

1. People can't be fixed. Helped and supported yes, but not fixed. **We're not machines. Always remember that.**
2. **People's history may be a mystery**, but it can reveal why they behave the way they do. Show an interest in people's past and you could help them in the present.
3. Most people suffer from S.A.D.S. – Self-Awareness Deficiency Syndrome. If you think you've not got it you probably have. **So be open to feedback. It could be a real gift to you.**

4. **Some people won't change. They don't want to.** They're lightbulbs. Unless you find the right switch. That's reality.

5. Intelligent people do stupid things. A high IQ does not mean automatic success with people. **They don't give out degrees in common sense.** So be humble.

6. Remember, you get what you tolerate. **Your silence speaks. But not always the message you want**. So speak up sometimes.

7. **Change is complicated.** People have their own reasons why they respond the way they do, and not all responses to change are negative.

8. **Humiliation is for amateurs. It's a sign of weakness, not power.** Get help if you need to. And take humiliation for a very, very long hike.

9. Being nice won't always work. Sorry to be a pain, but it won't. **But being unpopular may be the right way to be. Sometimes.** And that shows strength.

10. Remember, one person can make a difference, but it takes two to tango. **Have the courage to ask yourself if you're contributing to the problem.** That's brave. It's also incredibly helpful.

11. If you're not making the investments don't expect a return. **Money doesn't grow on trees and relationships don't survive on indifference.** That's the deal until you start making some deposits.

12. **Set your expectations high, but make them realistic.** That's unless you're addicted to stress. And that's not OK.

13. **Let sleeping dogs lie sometimes.** But make that an option, not a lifelong strategy. OK?

14. **Check out your attitude.** It's more important than you'll ever realize, and could rescue a relationship. Just ask Mark.

15. **Hang up your need to always be right.** You delude yourself when you believe you always are. You're not. So be willing to be wrong and then see how much real success you achieve.

16. Treat people as they want to be treated. You'd be surprised how much you gain when you first help people get what they want. **Treating everyone the same is naïve. So be flexible if you want to be successful.**

17. **Change can be scary,** but there are five simple ways you can make it more likely to succeed.

18. **When you know what's going on in people's world and what's important to them you're building a better relationship.** When you listen to understand and communicate your perspective you're on the way to building a brilliant one. That's to be desired.

19. **When you talk about *what worked well* and *even better if* . . . you're making your words count, not crucify.** That can resurrect people's confidence and redeem a relationship. That's powerful.

20. **When you work out why they're whinging you'll realize there are often reasons for people's resistance.** They need to be listened to, not labelled. That's respect.

21. **People need to feel S.P.E.C.I.A.L. because we're all important.** And when you meet that need you really do help people succeed. That's a privilege.

22. When people feel down you can help them up. You may need to reframe failure, go for quick wins and allow them time to feel down. For a while. **But that's just one chapter of the story. You can help them write a new one.** That's exciting.

23. Make sure you're heard. **Talk so people listen. You've got a message to bring.** Don't lose it in the detail. Bring it alive with facts but don't forget the feelings. Engage, influence and motivate.

And that my friend is how you succeed with people.

I wish you well in applying these ideas both in and outside the workplace.

About Paul McGee

Hi there. Here's some stuff about the guy who wrote this book.

My journey has been somewhat of a rollercoaster rather than a fairy tale. From working as a probation officer in West Yorkshire to managing a group of 30 women in a beefburger factory in East Anglia, life has definitely been varied.

Things changed rather dramatically when I lost my job through ill health aged just 24. I became ill with ME, or chronic fatigue syndrome, and found myself on invalidity benefit with a walking stick as a companion.

It took me a few years to fully recover, and during that time I set up my own business – being my own boss was the easiest way to manage my symptoms and the hours I worked.

Over these last 30 years I've established myself as a conference speaker, author and coach (check out www.theSUMOguy.com for more info). However, the journey to where I'm now at has been littered with challenges and disappointments, but through a combination of hard work, luck and the support of others, I've achieved a few successes too.

I am fortunate to have travelled the world through my work. I've spoken in over 40 countries across five continents and discovered that although we all have our cultural differences, there's so much that unites us. Wherever I go, it seems people have a common desire to learn about topics related to change, self-leadership, resilience, well-being, and communication. At the heart of this desire is one crucial theme. Relationships. Relationships with ourselves and others.

In 2019, I was awarded the title of Visiting Professor by the University of Chester in recognition of the extensive work I've done to make academic knowledge relevant, accessible, and practical in helping people from all background and ages – including school children. If I'm honest I still feel shocked to have received this title, and I understood where a friend of mine was coming from when they said, "What are you a professor in – common sense?" I get their point.

Apart from speaking and writing I spread my ideas and insights via most social media platforms. You can find me @theSUMOguy on Instagram, X, and TikTok, or connect on LinkedIn and Facebook. I would love it if you did.

In my spare time I enjoy being outdoors, preferably when it's warm, watching comedy, and following Wigan Athletic and Bradford City (it's a long story).

Helen, my wife of 35+ years is my best mate, and my two children Matt and Ruth are my biggest source of joy (closely followed by my cats Louis and Milo).

Finally, I am the least practical person you are likely to ever meet and was recently described as DIY intolerant.

More Books by Paul McGee

Self-Confidence: The Remarkable Truth of How a Small Change Can Make a Big Difference, 10th Anniversary edn, Capstone Publishing, 2019.

S.U.M.O Shut Up, Move On, The Straight Talking Guide to Creating and Enjoying a Brilliant Life, 10th Anniversary edn, Capstone Publishing, 2015.

S.U.M.O. Your Relationships: How to Handle Not Strangle the People You Live and Work With, Capstone Publishing, 2007.

How to Speak So People Really Listen, Capstone Publishing, 2016.

How to Have a Great Life: 35 Surprisingly Simple Ways to Success Fulfillment & Happiness, Capstone Publishing, 2018.

Yesss! The SUMO Secrets to Being a Postive, Confident Teenager, (illustrated by Fiona Osborne), Capstone Publishing, 2020.

The Happiness Revolution: A Manifesto for Living Your Best Life, (co-authored with Andy Cope), Capstone Publishing, 2021.

How Not To Worry: The Remarkable Truth of How a Small Change Can Help You Stress Less and Enjoy Life More, Capstone Publishing, 2012.

Index

7 Habits of Highly Effective People (Covey) 220

90/90 rule 218–20

accomplishment, importance of 208
actions, feelings following 209–10
"adrenaline addicts" 66
age, generational differences 22–3
anger 58, 158, 182
appreciation, showing 197–9
assertiveness, avoiding 113, 114
"attention awareness" 118
attention, being the centre of 136–7
attitude towards others 118–26
audience, engaging 216–17, 218

"B.M.W.s" (people who Bitch, Moan and Whinge) 173
background of a person *see* history of a person
bias, in-built 89
black and white thinking 12, 90, 130
blinkered approach 90–1, 128
brain function 120
Brown, Derren 106
Brown, Phil 76

cared for, helping people feel 149–50
CareerTrack 54–5
Carlyle, Thomas 208
certainty, need for 65–6
Chambers, Harry 55
change
  certainty of 62
  challenges of 64–5
  embracing 62–4
  leading to loss of status 66–8
  of location, benefits of 210–11
  and loss of control 68–9
  making a success 142–51
  past experiences of 70–1
  reasons people resist 65–72
  resistance due to past experience 23–4
  resistance to 42–6
  seen as a threat 65–6

childhood, describing 30–1
children
  investing time with 97–8
  lack of confidence 176
  rebelliousness 68
  relationship with own 97–8, 138–9, 198
choice
  and change 62, 63, 64, 65
  and control 148
clarity, giving 142–4, 214–15
coaching 40, 48, 224
communication
  clarity of message 220–1
  engaging your audience 218
  first impressions 218–20
  learning to speak 223–4
  problem before solution 221–3
  three common mistakes 214–18
  of your perspective 159–60
competence
  confidence rooted in 145–6
  developing people's 144–5
Confessions of a Conjuror (Brown) 106
confidence
  clarity creating 144
  lack of, and negativity 175–6
  nurturing 145–7
conflict 88–91
constructive criticism, giving 164–9
control
  and change 63, 65
  and choice 148
  giving others 147–8
  loss of, change leading to 68–9
conversations
  begin with the end in mind 220–1
  investing time in face-to-face 94–5, 149–50
  tough, listening to understand 157–8
courtesy 192–4
Covey, Dr. Stephen 220
Covid 19 pandemic 144, 148
  and change in work practices 28, 63–4
  effect on young people 28–9
  and need for clarity 144
criticism, giving 164–9
cultural differences 4
curiosity vs judging people 32
cynicism 24, 70–1

decisions
  deciding not to address an issue 112–14
  emotions taking over rational 49–51
  and negative people 177–8
detail, drowning people in 214–16
determination 128, 129
devil's advocate, playing 78–9
diplomacy 84, 164, 168, 207

emotions
  clouding your judgement 48–51
  danger of wallowing in 205
  vs logic, resistance to change 69–70
  see also feelings
encouragement 188–90
  and change 146, 147

in childhood 30, 204
of self-reflection 37
to challenge your views 131–2
Evans, Rachel Held 24
expectations, high but realistic 107–109
experiences, previous, effect on behaviour 23–4

facts vs feelings 131, 133–4, 217, 223
failure
in communicating 216–17
reframing 205–206
"Faulty Thinking" 222–3
feedback
learning to give 164–70
receiving 37–8, 158–9, 205–206, 224, 226
feelings
appealing to, persuasion 217
and facts 131, 217, 223
not always trusting 130–1, 132–3
right actions following 209–10
see also emotions
Ferguson, Sir Alex 18–20
first impressions 131, 218–20
flaws, embracing 109
flexibility in treatment of others 4–5, 13–14, 112, 136–40
focus 128
Franklin, Benjamin 62
"Fruity Thinking" 223

generational differences 23
goals of others, meeting 184–5
gut feeling, not always trusting 130–1

"halo effect" 119
history of a person 18–20
and age 22–3
awareness of helping you to understand 21
effect of the pandemic 28–9
previous experiences 23–4
previous work culture 29
shaping present behaviour 31–2, 33
upbringing 29–31
Hitler, Adolf 129
"horns effect" 119
humiliation 74–80
humility 45, 69, 128, 130

ideas
open to challenge 130
others' accepting your 194
important, seven ways to make people feel 182–202
indifference 100, 197
injustice, perceived sense of 177–8
intelligent people, mistakes made by 48–51
interest in people, showing 195–7
investment
of time in relationships 94–100
in yourself 223–4
irrational thinking 48–50

Jackson, Jesse 204
Jobs, Steve 6, 194–5

judgemental of others, avoid being 32, 90, 109

King, Martin Luther Jr 217
knowledge 7, 39

labels for negative people 172–3
leadership traits 128–9
learning
failure as part of 205–206
training, investing in 223–4
letting sleeping dogs lie 112–15
"lightbulb" behaviour 42–6
listening
openness to others' views 132–4
and showing interest 196–7
to understand 157–9, 199–201
location, changing 210–11
logic vs emotions 50

management style 29, 82–3, 94
McGee, Paul 235–7
books by 239–40
meetings
begin with the end in mind 220–1
keeping short 215–16
mistakes, communication 214–18
"mood hoovers" 173
motivation
quick wins helping 208–10
what motivates people 140

needs of others, meeting 139, 184–5
negative attitude towards someone
changing 122–6
focusing on 119–21
negativity 172–9
neurodiversity 39
niceness, problems with 82–5
non-action, impact of 57–8

one-size-fits-all approach, avoiding 13, 112
one-to-one conversations 149–50, 156
opinions, accepting others 131–2
overreacting 50–1

pandemic *see* Covid 19 pandemic
performance, small gestures improving 94
personalized treatment of others 186–8
perspective
communicating clearly 159–60
see also viewpoint
pessimism 172–9
pigeonholing people 131
politics 128–9
popularity/being liked, need for 83–5
positives, looking for 120, 125–6, 206–207
predictability, need for 65–6
presentations
begin with the end in mind 220–1
reducing length of 215–16
previous experiences

of change 70–2
factor in person's history 23–4
progress vs perfection 146, 209–10

questions to ask yourself 154–61
quick-fix solutions 12–13, 14
quick wins, going for 208–10

rational thinking, lack of 48–50
realistic expectations 107–109
relationships
family 97–8, 138–9
four questions to ask 154–61
investing time in 95–100
resistance to change, five reasons for 65–72
respect
and courtesy 192–3
vs popularity/being liked 84–5
Robinson, Anne, *The Weakest Link* 104, 105
Rockwell, Dan 157

S.A.D.S.(Self-Awareness Deficiency Syndrome) 36–9
S.P.E.C.I.A.L. acronym 182–202
"saving face" 77, 79
self-awareness, lack of 36–9
self-fulfilling prophecy, negative attitude 119–20
Self Confidence (McGee) 132
serving others 183–5
setbacks, helping people recover from 204–11
Sharma, Robin 83–4
silence, negative effect of 56, 57–8
spin 88–90
standards, maintaining own 107, 109
storytelling 88–90, 222
strengths 128, 129–30
stress 50–1
stubbornness 45, 128, 129
stupidity 48–51, 77, 129, 133
SUMO (Shut Up, Move On) questions 104, 209, 221–3
support, questions to ask 207

talking
about what worked well, feedback 167, 168
so people listen 214–24
see also communication
Thatcher, Margaret 128–9
thick skinned, being 78
tiredness 48–9
tolerance of behaviour 54–9
let sleeping dogs lie 112–15
training 223–4
treatment of others
in a personalized way 186–8
flexibility in 4–5, 13–14, 112, 136–40

U-turns, making 128–9
uncertainty 66, 130
underperformance, tolerating 55, 56–7

unrealistic expectations 105–106, 108, 109
upbringing 29–31

valuing people 156, 182–90, 197–8
viewpoint
challenging your own 133–4
reasons for not wanting to change 44–6
understanding someone else's 158–9
Vistage 166

Weakest Link, The (TV quiz show) 104–105, 107
weakness(es)
avoid mentioning 164–5
niceness exploited as 84
overused strength becoming 129–30
willingness to be wrong 128–34
work culture, effect of previous 29

Yancey, Philip 197

Ziglar, Zig 184